~Real Estate~

The World's Greatest Wealth Builder

The best-selling author tells how to make millions with "NO DOWN PAYMENT"

Carleton H. Sheets

Bonus Books, Inc., Chicago

02 01 00 99   5 4 3 2

Library of Congress Cataloging-in-Publication Data

Sheets, Carleton H.
    Real estate, the world's greatest wealth builder :
the best-selling author tells how to make millions
with "no down payment" / Carleton H. Sheets.
        p.   cm.
    Includes index.
    ISBN 1-56625-111-7 (pbk.)
    1. Real estate investment.   I. Title.
HD1382.5.S467   1998
332.63'247—dc21   98-35500
                                                                      CIP

Bonus Books, Inc.
160 East Illinois Street
Chicago, Illinois 60611

Printed in the United States of America

This book is dedicated to the tens of thousands of people from all walks of life, from all areas of the country, who have ordered my No Down Payment real estate home study course, and used it to enrich their lives, both financially and emotionally. In their letters and phone calls, they tell me about a better lifestyle, more self confidence, and greater self esteem. This is truly a harvest of new skills and knowledge, planted in the rich soil of opportunity in America. Included in this group are my wife, Shkora, my daughter, Cindy, and my son, Rick. My hat's off to every one of them.

Author note: Those of you who know me, already know I strongly believe in providing affordable housing. And, like me, the good folks at Habitat for Humanity believe in helping families to own their own home—whenever and wherever possible.

I wish to continue to support Habitat in their very worthwhile efforts. So I am donating all of my proceeds from the sale of this book to Habitat for Humanity International.

Contents

Preface

Throughout the pages of this text, the name of the Professional Education Institute will appear many times. This is the group that has marketed and distributed my home study program for the past 15 years, and they continue to do so today. In return for their fine assistance, their ethical standards, and their genuine care for the customer group they serve, I have given them exclusive rights to distribute all of my courses and programs.

What is their role related to this book? You may contact me through them. You may order my course or related materials through them. You may call them at 1-800-369-6314.

Foreword

In the early 1950s, William Zeckendorf made real estate history when he dismantled and sold the Empire State building. He didn't actually take the building apart and sell it piece by piece — he did it from a legal standpoint. He portioned off everything that had value: the building, personal property, leasehold interests, even the air rights — then sold them all separately, on paper, to investor groups.

Zeckendorf made millions from that one transaction and perhaps, unknowingly, started a whole new trend for creatively buying and selling real estate.

Donald Trump, Ted Turner, Trammel Crow, and a host of other "big hitters" use creative investing principles for acquiring real estate, businesses, and public corporations. This elite brand of entrepreneurs operate in a rarefied atmosphere that most of us would find difficulty in understanding.

"How does this relate to me?" you might ask.

Even though you and I may not have Harvard MBAs, and we're not out to acquire large hotels, develop shopping centers, or take over a movie studio, we do have immediate goals for our financial futures. The same creativity and techniques the movers and shakers of the world use to achieve their goals can be used at our level too.

As everyday real estate investors we **are** developing cash flows — not in the hundreds of millions of dollars per year, but easily in the low to middle six figures. And net worth? Not in the billions of dollars but many, many, many times in the million dollars-plus range. And by accomplishing this, we are putting ourselves ahead of 99 percent of the rest of the folks in this country.

Okay, time for a second *"How?"*: *"How can I do this?"*

Here's the simple, honest answer: "Get started with this book."

I want you to rise to the top 1 percent, and I want to help you get there. I want to show you how I (and many others) did it. I want to be your catalyst for success. I want to be your mentor. I want to lead you into the exciting field of real estate investing where you'll have more fun than you could ever imagine and make more money than you ever dreamed possible.

Thirty years ago, when I was first starting out, I was an absolute amateur investor. This book would have been enormously helpful to me back then.

Today, because of all the deals I've done, all the books I've read, all the seminars and courses I've taken and yes, because of the mistakes I've made along the way — I consider myself to be somewhat of an expert in the field of creative real estate investing. And I can positively help you avoid making many of the same mistakes I made along the way.

I can't take credit for many of the creative techniques the Trumps and the Turners of the world (and I) have used, but I will take a small amount of credit for condensing these techniques so the average person can use them on a daily basis.

Buying real estate creatively is not a get-rich-*quick* program (although some of my students would disagree). But it is a get-rich program!

If you have average intelligence, can read, write, and do simple math, you already possess much of what it takes to get started. *You* must supply the desire, ambition, and some well thought-out goals. *I'll* supply the final ingredient: The knowledge and the "know-how." That's the role this book plays.

You hold in your hands all that it takes for you to get started realizing your dreams. Take it home, study it — put it into action. The ride to the top is fun and well worth the effort.

I know . . . I've been there!

CHAPTER ONE

We Are Who We Are . . . And Here's Who I Am

Sometimes, "glamorizing" tends to creep in when an author writes about himself. Either he claims that he was born in a log cabin which he himself built, and then triumphed over impossible adversities . . . or he claims he was an Oxford graduate at the age of 10. Sorry, my history is quite normal . . . as you're about to see.

I WAS BORN!

At least two major events occurred in the year 1939, one of which was *very* important to me:

1. World War II broke out.
2. I was born.

Oh, actually a lot of other things were happening. I understand New York was hosting a big World's Fair, the centerpieces of which were the Trylon and Perisphere (remnants of which still exist, I'm told).

Franklin D. Roosevelt was in his second term. *Gone With the Wind* was a box office smash. The poet William

Butler Yeats and Pope Pius XI died. Probably other kids were born too, but I didn't know any of them.

My place of birth was Olney, Illinois. That's a small town in the southern part of the state, not far from the Indiana border — real Norman Rockwell mid-America, with tall corn and pink cheeks and nobody having to lock the car, or even the front door, at night.

My father's ancestry was Welsh and German; my mother's was German and Scotch. I guess that makes me something of a mutt. But you can tell from those roots: They were conservative in both politics and in their personal outlook on life.

Not that this was bad. They never got wild and crazy, and they cared about education and manners. They also were both educated and cultured: They had met when both were violinists with the Springfield, Illinois, Symphony Orchestra.

My earliest recollections of my father are a little hazy. He worked for a while for Procter & Gamble, and his job had him on the road several nights a week. So my mother was the more influential parent during my early years.

And memories of those times are happy ones. Despite the fact that Hitler was laying waste to half of Europe; and Mussolini was storming into Albania and Ethiopia; and Francisco Franco was marching through Barcelona; and U-boats were sinking ships every day; and London had air raid sirens crying out doom every night; and the United States was calling up its best and healthiest young men in a military draft . . .

Despite all of this, none of it touched me. I was loved. I was cared for. I had lots of friends. The war? That was in a strange and forbidding place called Europe, and then, later, even stranger places called Asia and Japan. Besides, my dad had a medical deferment. He had broken his nose playing baseball as a kid and had breathing problems. I'm sure he was grateful later in life for that errant pitch. So all of the war "stuff" was distant.

THE EARLY YEARS

When I was six years old, my brother, David, was born. The gap between us wasn't a generation, but to a six-year-old it might as well have been.

Oh, he was never in the way, but a subtle change took place: Now we were a full-fledged "family," not just a threesome. So planning took on a family tone.

For example, when I was nine and my brother was three, we started taking summer vacations. (Odd: I now think of almost every moment in Olney as a kind of vacation on its own!) It was the vacations that first opened my eyes to the mysterious word "budgeting," a word and a concept that never seems to affect kids of any economic status before they're eight or nine (and to some, a totally foreign concept even as adults).

My dad was of the old-fashioned school: Mothers didn't work outside the home. So he gave Mom a fixed amount of money each week. It was up to her to spread that money around to cover food and utilities and clothes for the family and repairs. She kept money for each purpose in separate envelopes hidden in a clothes drawer. Then there was one envelope labeled "Vacation." That envelope got the unused money, if any, from the other envelopes. I can still see my mother's neat writing on those envelopes.

Somehow my mother was able to sock away $200 to $300 in that vacation envelope every year. That doesn't sound like much today, when it can cost $300 for me to fly from my home in Florida to Atlanta. But in the late 1940s, when we could buy a new car for under a thousand dollars, send a letter first-class for 3 cents, and buy a thick juicy

steak for less than a dollar and a loaf of bread for a dime . . .
well, $200 to $300 could finance a pretty comfortable vacation, especially for a family with a couple of kids from Olney, Illinois.

One year we went to Cape Cod; another, to the Wisconsin Dells; another, to the Ozark Mountains; and still another to Daytona Beach. It was during the trip to Daytona
that I lost my heart to Florida . . . and even at that young
age I made a silent vow to myself to move, some day, to
that tropical paradise.

BYE, BYE, OLNEY!

In 1949, my father's company transferred him to another small town — Delaware, Ohio. The biggest problem
with Delaware, Ohio, was telling people we lived in Delaware. Unless they were from the same region, we'd get a
"Huh?" reaction.

Since then, I've met people from Louisiana, Missouri.
I've met people from four different Mexicos — Mexico,
Maine; Mexico, Missouri; Mexico, New York; and the real
Mexico. So the idea of Delaware, Ohio, isn't so strange any
more. But people still look at me in a confused way when I
tell them I spent most of my young life in Delaware, Ohio.

Actually, I liked Delaware. The town was about the
same size as Olney, with the same warm, friendly, neigh-
borly people. But for the first time, I became aware that I
wasn't cut of quite the same piece of cloth as the other
kids in town. I wasn't making friends as easily as everybody thought I should. I was the new kid on the block. I
was shy and sensitive. And that gave me the notion that I
was lacking in self-confidence. (You know the feeling: The
more you believe you're lacking self-confidence, the more
self-confidence you lack.) And I regarded myself as a seri-

ous thinker. This gave me a rationale and an excuse for being something of a loner.

Then something hit me that made adjusting to the new town even tougher. Just as our first summer in Delaware was beginning — pow! Down I came with viral pneumonia.

Today, pneumonia isn't anywhere nearly as deadly as it was then. We have a host of "miracle" drugs. Then, pneumonia could be lethal. For nine weeks I lay in bed.

As Shakespeare said, "Sweet are the uses of adversity." I was as sick as any kid ever had been. But I had a big advantage: This was before the era of television. Day after day, lying in bed, I read. In fact, I read between 15 and 20 books during that illness, and this gave me a love of reading that persists even to this day.

Oh, yes, now we have television sets all over the house, and I thank television for giving me the exposure that makes a book like this possible, but here we are, during the Age of Television, in a *book* . . . my first love!

My big scare came when I was almost over my illness. I'd been in bed for nine weeks. My mother helped me out of bed, to go to the doctor's office. You can imagine how weak I was after more than two months of lying in a bed.

The doctor gave me a stern, serious look. He shook his head sadly. "I'm afraid I have some bad news," he told me. "You have a bad case of Bubblegumitis." It was his "cute" way of prefacing telling me I was almost well.

But in the weakened state I was in, I never even heard the last word. His serious demeanor and the gravity of his pronouncement were all I needed to start sobbing uncontrollably. I might never recover from so serious a malady!

My mother started laughing. That *really* set me off. How could she laugh, when I was at death's door with — what was it? — "Bubblegumitis"?

Oh, gee. Bubblegum. But even when I recognized the joke, I couldn't laugh for a while, because I had been so near the edge of panic. In fact, I remember sobbing in short staccato bursts as the "good" news crept into my consciousness. My mother was embarrassed by my outburst and apologized for my taking the joke so seriously.

The outcome of Bubblegumitis was a lesson I'm glad I learned. Until then, I don't think my sense of humor had really developed. This gave it a jump-start. Over the years, I've become more and more convinced that a healthy sense of humor not only will give anyone a better and happier life, but a better perspective on both personal matters and business. If you can temper a serious reaction with a sense of humor, you gain perspective . . . and respect and liking from others. That was what Bubblegumitis did for me, and I recommend it.

THE YOUNG ENTREPRENEUR

Slowly my energy levels returned to normal. And a few months later my parents suggested one way I could regain strength — and confidence — was by getting a job.

I'm sure, too, as I look back, that my working and paying for all of my small expenses and the cost of my clothes helped my mother fatten the "vacation envelope." An allowance? I never had one and didn't know the meaning of the word.

I thought cutting lawns would be a solid way of earning some money. I'd be out in the sunshine, I'd be exercising, and I had a good supply of potential customers because Delaware, Ohio, was a town of homes with lawns.

So I asked my mother if she would give me the money to buy a lawn mower. To her eternal credit, she said she would *loan* me the money; I could repay her, in installments, from the income I'd realize from that mower.

I don't think I'm editorializing when I say that I wish every young person could have that kind of exposure to financial responsibility. I don't think I'm preaching when I say that if every young person realized the give-and-take of life instead of just the take, we'd have a better society and less crime. I don't think I'm off-target when I say that young people who recognize early-on that the world doesn't owe them a living are the ones who become thoughtful leaders.

Anyway, I made that deal with my mother, and I was on my way, with my first independent business venture . . . and, for that matter, my first "deal" with no money down.

One benefit of being a young entrepreneur is the guidance we get, that serves us so well later on. We have business experiences that prevent us from making naive mistakes when, as adults, our decisions have much greater consequences.

For example, one day I was working hard for an elderly widow, raking her yard, picking up twigs and sticks, and weeding her garden. I worked steadily for more than four solid hours. She gave me $1.40 — about 35¢ an hour. I went home with tears in my eyes and complained to my mother about how unfair that was. Another valuable lesson! My mother told me that if I thought it was unfair, I should have talked to my customer directly and immediately, and not just complained at home. She said I should either go back and discuss the matter with the lady or just never work for her again.

I did what most kids would do. I chose the more diplomatic course and never went back to that woman's home. Was I right? Who knows? I wasn't an aggressive child, and the lesson in pragmatism took root slowly. Today, I probably would have said to my customer, "Are you kidding? I'm worth at least 40¢ an hour!"

Another lesson in pragmatism occurred a short time later (I was growing up fast!). I had a friend who lived about a block away. As youngsters do, we somehow got into an argument which wound up in a fistfight. He punched me in the nose. Again I went home with tears in my eyes, and again my mother's comments struck home: "If you can't defend yourself, you shouldn't be fighting."

You know what? That's good *business* advice, too!

DIFFERENT ISN'T ALWAYS BETTER

I continued to feel like an outsider in school. One reason for my lack of confidence was that my wardrobe consisted of many hand-me-downs. My source of clothing was a cousin in Chicago, about two years older than I was. When he outgrew his latest shirts and pants and coats, down they came to me.

This in itself wasn't all that unusual. What set me apart was *style*. People in urban Chicago had a dress-code on a plane different from that in the rural community of Delaware, Ohio. I'd show up wearing knickers, when all the other boys were wearing jeans. I was unique, and not in a very pleasant way.

Another way in which I felt unique was that I seemed to be working harder than anyone else within my circle of acquaintances. Oh, some of them had odd jobs. A few had paper routes, and some cut lawns. The girls babysat. But I always seemed to be busier — to have *more* lawns to cut.

And many of them had allowances, too. So when we went to the A&W Root Beer stand across from the cemetery, I didn't feel comfortable ordering a 25-cent hamburger. I would sip my five-cent draft of root beer and stare hungrily at their sandwiches. Maybe, though, as I think back, frugality dictated the choice more than financial circumstance — a frugality that came from my being responsible for my own expenses . . . my financial destiny, if you will.

Not long after I started working on lawns I also got a paper route. That meant another no-money-down financial deal with my mother, this time for a bicycle.

(Incidentally, so there's no mistake, I repaid the money I borrowed for my various assets . . . and to this day I feel pretty good about it. When I hear stories of people who feel clever because they've been able to duck the responsibility of repaying money loaned to them, it literally makes me sick.)

The Sunday newspaper was (and still is) big and heavy. I couldn't carry all my papers on my bike. Here's where having understanding parents pays off! My dad would get up at 4:30 or 5:00 a.m. every Sunday morning to drive me around town, delivering the Sunday paper. He never complained. Now I wish I had been more vocally thankful than I was at the time.

THE MIDDLE-CLASS CHURCHGOER

Just about every friend I had at the time . . . and for that matter, just about every acquaintance . . . was someone I had met either in school or through my membership in the church youth group. I really enjoyed the church group and didn't think it was at all unusual to have achieved an almost perfect church attendance record, both in Olney and in Delaware.

Most of my friends shared my own economic circumstances. All of us were what might be called lower middle class to middle class. We didn't really associate with families of affluence. I had the notion that richer people had an edge over me — which they did, obviously, but only in the amount of money they could spend on material possessions — and that they just weren't as nice as my own group — which is the kind of automatic and senseless prejudice I'm glad I've outgrown.

My attitude, obviously, stemmed from my own up-bringing . . . and, I suspect, the upbringing my parents had had. We always had known that our lifestyle was lower down the economic ladder than the folks who lived in big houses and had domestic help. We rationalized. After all, that's what people do. We rationalized that affluence was equivalent to stinginess . . . to selfishness . . . and to general unhappiness with life.

I think it made us feel better to draw that conclusion, and even today — no, *especially* today — I see that same re-action among the financially disadvantaged. Now that I know better, it saddens me to think I once succumbed to such simplistic, unreasoning conclusions.

Now that I've joined the ranks of the affluent, I've come to a conclusion 180 degrees different from the one I had as a child. Most of the people I know who have "made it" are just the reverse of my original evaluation: They are warm, giv-ing, and generous. They care about society. They support local and civic ventures, whether it's the schools, the church, the library, the symphony orchestra, or a charitable organi-zation. It's those who live their lives in economic despera-tion who too frequently are bitter, selfish, and withdrawn.

I understand these attitudes and wish everyone could share my financial good fortune. (After reading this book, I'm convinced you will have a much more powerful op-portunity to achieve monetary riches. But I hope, too, that regardless of money, you are one of those who judges peo-ple as individuals and not as objects of a group prejudice.)

MY HIGH SCHOOL AND COLLEGE YEARS

At the age of 14 I "graduated" from mowing lawns and delivering newspapers. I became a busboy in a restaurant. I made the huge sum of 60¢ an hour! I remember looking at the wristwatch I had bought with my new wealth: Every time the second hand swept around the dial, I was one cent richer! Wow! Boy, was I proud.

I kept this job throughout high school and college, working 30 to 35 hours a week. I wasn't at all bothered by the number of hours — this was the marvelous work ethic my parents had superimposed on me — but I do remember that I didn't seem to have as much leisure time as many of my friends and acquaintances.

Whether being a workaholic contributed to my ongoing feelings of inadequacy (or the reverse), I don't know. I do know I was lacking in self-confidence. I remember how uneasy I was, not only one-to-one, but being around groups of people as well. How odd are the twists of life and fortune! Today, those who attend my seminars almost always comment on my ease of delivery and my self-confidence. Believe me, it's hard-earned . . . and believe me, it certainly is a factor of success in the moneymaking field this book will describe to you.

But don't be concerned. If you, like me (or the "me" of my younger years), lack self-confidence, that situation easily is overcome when you do what I'll tell you to do in this book. It's coming up!

When I say "hard-earned" I mean that I was lucky to recognize lack of self-confidence as a major personal deficiency. I resolved to do something about it. I deliberately chose a curriculum that would challenge me. I took speech courses. I became a member of my high school's debating and extemporaneous speaking teams. I became active in dramatics.

(Let me suggest this same course of action if you have a youngster who gives off signals of inadequacy. You can re-shape his or her future. I also have a profound admiration for adults who join Toastmasters, a national organization devoted to perfecting public speaking techniques and in-creasing self-esteem and improving communicative skills.)

I don't recall being the champion debater or being a noted Shakespearean actor. I certainly do recall, though, that sticking to these activities and this discipline (however uncomfortable I was with them), even after going on to col-lege, finally achieved what I had hoped to achieve: I had the self-confidence to talk on equal terms with almost *any-body*, in *any* discussions or areas of interest.

Working in that same restaurant for seven long years, first as a busboy and later as a waiter, was an extraordinar-ily valuable character-building experience for me. I learned to accept hard work, not only as a fact of life but as an as-set of life. I learned not only to become self-disciplined, but I also learned the value of self-discipline.

I learned the danger of expecting handouts without giving anything in return. As I said earlier, whatever money I needed for clothes (an advantage of working: I had moved beyond hand-me-downs) or movies or dates, I had to earn. As a waiter, I learned that the size of my tips was directly related to my own efficiency, courtesy, and respectfulness . . . without appearing to be subservient.

What wonderful lessons! I treasure them. I'm grateful for having had them. I'm convinced that such experiences have a profound effect on our adult lives.

I absolutely believe in being nice to people.

I absolutely believe in being polite.

I absolutely believe in being appreciative for what we get, from life and from other people.

I absolutely believe in treating others with dignity and respect.

I absolutely believe in being one's self, not falsely posturing and trying to be or act more than you are.

And, I absolutely believe in the importance of budgeting money and keeping expenditures in line with one's earnings. I admonish young people: "Don't tell me how much you make; tell me how much you save." This, in fact, is the core of success in real estate investing.

I think if you discuss my lifestyle and methods with others who know me, they will verify that I've carried these concepts into adulthood, strongly and proudly.

EARLY BUSINESS HISTORY: I JOIN CORPORATE AMERICA

When I graduated from college in 1961 (I had worked as a waiter right up to graduation), it was a golden time for bright, young recent graduates. Many big corporations were aggressively looking for us. The number of graduates wasn't as large as it is today. Can you believe it? I interviewed with nearly 50 major companies, and from those interviews I was offered 14 or 15 jobs. After consideration, I accepted a job with Armstrong Cork Company. They paid me the magnificent sum of $415 a month. I was in the chips!

I had fallen in love and married during my final year of college. Now, as an aspiring young businessman, I entered the Armstrong training program and was assigned to San Francisco, where I was "stationed" for two years. I was then transferred to Raleigh, North Carolina, as "resident salesman."

My daughter, Cindy, was born in San Francisco. Rick was born in Raleigh. We became a complete family with all the joys and tribulations attached to such a close entity. In fact, I sometimes think about "raising children" when people ask me about problems connected with real estate investing. Are there problems? Sure there are. But, like raising a family, the rewards are so great the problems take a back seat. If your children are still "kids" trust me on this one. My children are now adults . . . and our continued closeness and the pride I feel for them both are really beyond description.

In Raleigh, my job was to sell the metal caps (called crowns) that fit onto soft drink bottles. The resident sales manager told me that even though I was still fairly new with the company and was only 23 years old, Armstrong Cork considered me an "up-and-comer." My job folder indicated to him that I was responsible — a self-starter. That evaluation stayed with me throughout my four years in Raleigh, because not only did I enjoy remarkable success, besting the previous sales record by 25 percent, but gradually the company let me operate more and more independently of direct management.

After four years, Armstrong transferred me to Atlanta, where I had major responsibility: Marketing liaison with the Coca-Cola Company. No, I'm wrong about that. I didn't really have the responsibility. Here I was under constant supervision by the district office management. No more independence. I became more and more "itchy," because I began to realize that I wasn't really suited for a role in some corporate hierarchy.

But, as you can imagine, I was making good money and wasn't inclined to break away from corporate America; I *was*, however, discontented enough to think I wanted to break away from my current job.

So I accepted an offer to become Director of Marketing — a job that had all kinds of executive overtones — for Lykes Pasco Packing Company in Dade City, Florida. I had never forgotten my goal of wanting to live in Florida. This new job brought a dual satisfaction to me: I could live in

the land of my dreams and I had a better job with more responsibility. This company was, at that time, the biggest
orange juice processor in the world. And I was the Director
of Marketing, with a nice boost in title and salary.

A mistake. I admit now, I was too young and too inex-
perienced for this job. I hung in there, but this was a sophisticated marketer that couldn't accept any less than
perfect performance. A little less than two years after I'd
joined the company, they fired me.

PANIC TIME . . . AND THE BEST THING THAT EVER HAPPENED TO ME!

Have you ever been fired? Many of us have, at one
time or another. Whether deserved or not, getting fired is a
terrible blow to the ego, self-confidence, and self-esteem.

I had been "the bright young executive" . . . and suddenly I was the out-of-work incompetent. Daily, hourly —
panic grew. My self-esteem was dropping to zero. Discour-
agement was turning to panic.

And yet, never for a moment did it occur to me that I
couldn't do *something* to earn a decent living to support my
family. The truth staring me in the face was that I *knew* my
future could not be with a major corporation. I had seen my
father working, working, working. Over a 40-year span he
had worked for only two companies. Finally, at age 58, the
company he was working for told him that he was going to
be "retired early." This would entitle him to a pension
check of *$92 a month* . . . when he reached age 65. Whew!

Not for me.

So, for about two months I looked into opportunities
that would allow me to go into business for myself. I exam-
ined an orange juice distributorship (after all, I had spent
two years as Director of Marketing for an orange juice

company). I looked into the possibility of owning and running a paint brush manufacturing company. I thought of taking over a small restaurant. I explored the potentials of several partnerships in the distribution business.

Then, an old friend from Armstrong Cork, who had become a real estate broker in Tampa, urged me to get into real estate. Real estate? What did I know about real estate?

Well, the rest, as they say . . . and as you'll see in the next chapter of this book . . . is history!

CHAPTER TWO

The Oh-So-Sweet Uses of Adversity

*What's the benefit of looking into "How I did it"? I hope that for you, the benefit is this realization: No magic was involved. No big talent was involved. No huge stroke of luck was involved. The word that describes my entry into the immensely profitable world of real estate investing is **logic.** Logic underlies every step and every facet of real estate investing. That's why I invite you, with complete sincerity and confidence: Come on in, the water's fine!*

MY FIRST EXPERIENCE IN REAL ESTATE PROFITS

The germ of my entry into real estate was an enlightening "experience" I had when I was in San Francisco, working for Armstrong Cork.

We rented an apartment and lived in it for about a year. After my first child, Cindy, was born, I began thinking about a more homelike ambiance. I heard of a property for sale and went to look at it. It turned out to be a nice little house with three bedrooms and two baths, in a desirable neighborhood.

The house was on the market for $18,250. (Try finding a tar-paper shack for that amount today!) It had an assumable VA loan at 4.5 percent.

Problem: I needed $3,000 for a down payment. At the time the total sum of my liquid assets was about $600. So what else to do but . . . call my dad.

My folks didn't have much money either, but what they did have was excellent credit. My father agreed to help negotiate a loan. What he did, in effect, was lend me his credit. Neither one of us put up cash out of our own pockets . . . not that we could.

So I bought the house, lived in it for a year, and sold it for $23,500. After paying back the $3,000 loan I suddenly had more cash than I'd ever had in my life — over $5,000.

I used the profit from that home as a down payment on the house I bought in Raleigh, when we moved there for my next assignment. A few years later, when I was transferred to Atlanta, I sold that house and made a profit of about $5,000. With my winnings I bought a house in Atlanta. Each move in my early odyssey turned out to be profitable . . . at least, from a real estate point of view.

At the time, I didn't analyze the results as well as I should have. If I had, I'd have realized that I made more money buying and selling real estate, without even having a master plan, than I'd ever have been able to save in twice the amount of time by renting and trying to salt some money away. If I had, I'd have quit my job and become a full time real estate investor.

Eventually, two shining lessons became clear to me: People have made more money just buying a home to live in than they could make through any other legal endeavor; and by buying real estate and holding it, *tremendous* profits are possible as the property appreciates in value and the mortgage is paid down.

I have always dreamed of accumulating a substantial amount of wealth and I always knew that real estate was the way to accomplish my dream.

While I have substantially increased my net worth, your training allowed me to do more than just fatten my pockets. I have utilized this knowledge to benefit some of my less fortunate loved ones.

Because I took your course, my wife's sister and her five children enjoy a four bedroom home in a stable neighborhood. She is able to rent this home from us at considerably less than the market rate, yet we still have a positive cash flow.

My brother and his wife and four children now enjoy a four-bedroom home which we recently purchased. Through utilizing your techniques I showed my brother how he could lease-option this property from me, yet keep his monthly out-flow of cash at the same level that was required for the two bedroom home he was living in.

I have done many things in my life that have given my mother reason to be proud of me. But her response to seeing the home in which I placed my brother and his family has convinced me that this tops them all.

I don't know how to thank you for what your course has done for me, and this is just the beginning! It gets better every day.

— *Robert Hardy III,*
Missouri

Get this: The home I bought and sold all those years ago in San Francisco is now worth more than $325,000.

"WHY NOT GO INTO REAL ESTATE?"

What kind of question is that — "Why not go into real estate?" When that question first was posed to me, I more or less was puzzled. To me, it paralleled asking me, "Why don't you go to Africa and become a lion hunter?" I was about equally prepared for either endeavor.

But when my old friend from Armstrong Cork suggested I get into real estate, a light bulb flickered on. I remembered how well I had done, buying and selling my homes during the various corporate transfers I had made: Very profitable!

So okay, I thought, let's give it a shot.

I didn't have any self-employment opportunities or red-hot job offers, so I made the big decision. Within a couple of months I had my real estate license. Understand, please: I really wasn't interested in real estate as a career; I *was* just interested in being self-employed. Self employment suggested being able to make my own decisions . . . keeping the money I earned . . . being able to dictate my own working hours . . . not having an external boundary or limit on my progress or my future. That's what made the idea worth a try.

Over the years, I have espoused the benefits of self-employment, literally all over the world. And, as you'd expect, I've seen mixed results. Some folks are just not psychologically equipped to be in business for themselves. They want someone else to tell them what to do. They fear having to make a decision. When they do have to make a decision, they agonize over it for days before they make it and for days after they make it. When they make a mistake, it's cosmic — the world is coming to an end.

So they procrastinate, make decisions reluctantly and late (or never), and develop a style that has them coming in *second* in the ongoing race for success. Self-employment isn't for them.

But for those with plain, old-fashioned guts, self-confidence, and the right knowledge, the future is limitless. I suggest you look in your mirror and ask yourself the basic question — not "Will I succeed?" or "What are the odds?" or "Is this a crowded field?" but "Am I capable of making a quick, hard decision and sticking to it and living by it and not looking backward with a mournful 'What if . . .' sob?" If you can give that mirror an enthusiastic "yes!", you could have a future whose limits don't even exist.

Is there a middle road? You bet! And you don't even have to call it self-employment. It is simply becoming a part-time real estate investor where you buy one single family rental home, or a two or four-family house — and then one more, and then one more. Are you working for yourself when you do this? Of course, but maybe you're more comfortable thinking about this activity just as a part-time endeavor, rather than self-employment, which carries all sorts of connotations about giving up economic life support systems.

So, let me pose the question to you that started this chapter: "Why Not Go Into Real Estate?" You can see now that you don't have to go into it full-time. In fact, the beauty of my system is that you can do it in your spare time, in just a few hours a week, and very quickly develop income and profits that far outweigh your salary or wages at your regular job. THEN, the decision to go into business for yourself, if you choose to do so, is quite easy!

FIRST SUCCESSES!

Launching my new career had the usual glitches and setbacks, but my enthusiasm at the notion of being my own boss held firm long enough to get my first listing — an apartment building.

Oh, how I tried to sell that building. For two weeks I called everybody I knew and everybody I didn't know. I published ads in the paper. I "pitched" other real estate agents. I used every technique, every sales approach, every angle I could think of.

Nothing!

Now I realize that two weeks is a very short time to sell a listing, but back then I rapidly became frustrated because I thought the apartment building represented such a good investment. Then it occurred to me: Why not buy it myself?

Since I didn't have any money and I didn't have any credit, I brought the idea to purchase the building to two friends. They had some dollars to invest (we only needed $6,000). They shared my view that the building was a good investment and we had better grab it before someone else did. Each of my two friends put up $3,000, and I took an ownership interest for putting the deal together.

When we sold that apartment building 18 months later, after some cosmetic improvement, we made a profit of $80,000. (And bear in mind, that was 1971. Back then you could buy a brand new Cadillac for $7,000!)

I had to ask myself, "How long has *this* been going on?" Never in my life had I made so much money in a single transaction.

The purchase and sale of that apartment building was a gigantic educational experience for me. I came to two cataclysmic decisions: a) I didn't really care for real estate brokerage and b) I had found my new career-home in real estate investing.

You can see the incentive: I had picked up a substantial amount of money without having invested one cent. Those who had put up the money also had profited well. And at no time was their investment in jeopardy, because it was protected by ownership of the building — a building that was going up in value and had a nice positive spendable cash flow.

THE MOMENTUM CONTINUES

Armed with success and a new jolt of self-confidence, I began putting together more partnerships. Each was easier than the ones before, because I was gradually building up an ongoing reputation for making money in real estate.

The partnerships became bigger and bigger. My personal involvement-specialty was "re-habbing" the properties — painting, plastering, landscaping, whatever it took. Within five years I created what I thought was an incredible fortune in real estate, in the Tampa area. At my peak, with partners, I owned almost 500 rental units.

As you yourself will discover, each succeeding transaction gets easier. That's one of the spectacular benefits of being a real estate investor: You can start off in high gear and then go faster and faster as your own experience sharpens your technique.

My reputation as a real estate investor began to grow, and after a couple of years, a local real estate education company asked me if I might be interested in teaching a course on the principles and practices of real estate. To whom? To prospective employees and agents coming into the business.

I agreed. A pleasant diversion. My classes were well-attended and my "students" were very responsive. I thought back to my introverted early school days and blessed the decision I had made to get involved in dramatics and speech-making and debating. What a strong background these gave me to teach the principles of real estate investing!

As an aside, the many and different success stories you see on my television program each year are not "students" from those early days of teaching. No, they are students who saw my show recently, ordered my home study course, put the principles into actions, and created tremendous financial wealth for themselves.

> There is no way I would have ever developed a $250,000 net worth in under two years, if not for your course. A quarter million dollars! Let alone create a $36,000 positive cash flow working four to five hours a week. It would probably take me 100 years to do that. Finally we have hope for our future (and our three kids) instead of just living paycheck to paycheck.
>
> — *Lawrence Danza, New York*

These same principles are outlined for you in this book. I do invite you to consider investing in my home study course if you feel you would benefit from having my system laid out for you in greater detail and depth, and with more techniques and examples. I also would have you consider owning it if you are someone who absorbs information more quickly when presented in audio or videotape format.

In either event, if you follow and apply the principles I will demonstrate here, you *will* succeed. And when you do, as I ask of all my students, I respectfully request that you let me know, and consider sharing your success with others. By doing this, you will motivate others to take the important step of improving their family's financial well-being. For years, I've been spreading the word with the help of important people just like you . . . and believe me, hundreds of thousands of people have benefited.

A DOWNHILL SLIDE . . . AND A RECOVERY

About five years after I became a serious real estate investor, I found my career spiraling downward. I lost nearly all the profits I had built up. What happened? Was my new career founded on air instead of solid ground?

The combination of overbuilding, the energy crisis (remember the long, snaking lines at every gas pump?), and my own wild inclination to buy *any* real estate that came along, with the right terms, regardless of location or actual investment potential, was deadly.

You know what that dismal episode reminds me of? Professional athletes. They typify "professional" people who come to feel that because they're successful in one field, they will be successful in any activity they enter. That was Carleton Sheets: I felt I could easily transfer my success to anything I wanted to do.

So I became involved in condominium conversions and development. I even had an interest in a big hotel in Tampa.

I grabbed every piece of property I could get my hands on, regardless of its potential or lack of potential.

I not only strayed from the formula that had brought me success, I darned near abandoned it altogether.

Eventually the smoke and fire cleared, and so did my vision. I realized how far I had wandered off the logical course I should have been following — the basic residential property formula I had perfected; the one that had served me so well.

But the recognition of what I had done wrong didn't overcome the sad economic reality of the situation.

Whew! Was the roof falling in? Here we were in the year 1976. I was 37 years old, supposedly the model of success, actually teaching others how to do what I did . . . and I was barely able to make the mortgage payment on my own home.

Do you know what I did to help put food on the table? I increased my teaching load.

(An aside: Ask *any* successful teacher of a professional subject about the benefits of teaching and one benefit you're sure to hear is, "No one learns like a teacher." The interplay, research, classroom presentation and questions, and even occasional heckling not only keeps us sharp, it forces us to stay abreast of what's going on in our field of interest.)

As I swung into my teaching career, I found I was really enjoying what I did. At the same time, I continued investing — albeit smarter! The standard litmus test — do you look forward to going to work? — resulted in a resounding yes.

I was a lot wiser than I had been. I had learned that rushing ahead blindly might result in short-term success but inevitably resulted in long-term disaster. It's like the gambler in Las Vegas who keeps winning and leaves his winnings on the table for the next bet. He can show a huge profit, but it's all on the table. Eventually he has to lose . . . and when he does, he's wiped out.

To be an effective teacher, one has to be organized. That means structured notes. Looking over my notes, I recognized the seeds of articles, books, and home study courses.

So I began to write articles. I began to write home study courses. Over the next three years, for the National Association of Realtors and the Real Estate Securities and Syndication Institute, I was the sole author or author-in-partnership for at least three separate complete courses. I learned that I really did like to write.

Since that time I have authored seven additional courses and books. I can tell you, a course or a book is more than an accomplishment; it is a symbol of dedication, of personal discipline (and, I hope, of knowledge).

BRINGING US UP TO DATE

Visualize this:

You have made a lot of money.

You have made it without proper analysis of how and why you made a lot of money.

You begin to lose money.

You ask yourself, "Why am I now losing money when, until now, I was making money?"

You analyze.

You understand what you did right and what you did wrong.

You assemble a new set of operating rules, with governors on the throttle and a more mature, more careful, more exact, more logical approach.

That's what I did.

The result was everything I could hope it to be. I modified my analysis and my negotiating techniques to conform to a system of business practices that included built-in safeguards. My income shot up and never quit.

When success comes like that, unlikely people take notice. As I closed in on a total of about $20 million in properties bought and sold . . . and kept refining my teaching techniques . . . I began to get offers to appear on radio and television shows. People were fascinated with the concept.

Of course, I couldn't explain in detail all the facets. I was terrified that some who heard and saw me would rush out and do what I had done originally — buy houses and apartment buildings without applying sets of standards and without having the necessary "book" knowledge that would prevent disaster. I didn't want to be the doctor who said to a television audience, "Exercise more," and then discover that half the audience had suffered severe exhaustion.

I wondered: How could I impart the total knowledge — not just the seductively attractive superficial highlights, but the totality of the experiences that had given me a unique knowledge of real estate investing?

The answer came in the most fortuitous way. An executive of the Professional Education Institute, an organization located in the Chicago suburb of Burr Ridge, Illinois, heard me speak. Hearing all the cautions and warnings I had included, and heeding my descriptions of the relatively easy and highly profitable results one might expect, he made two suggestions that literally changed my own personal history.

His first suggestion was that I "formalize" the information into a coordinated course of study.

His second suggestion was that I work with the Institute in preparing a half-hour television program to explain the course of study.

Both suggestions struck home.

The first suggestion made powerful sense because I could see that if I had a coordinated course of study, complete with audio cassettes my "students" could use as on-going references, plus a workbook they could use as a check-list, I could standardize my instruction. I wouldn't have to be standing right there. Many, many thousands who otherwise would have to devote two days to my live seminar could profit from the course. And I knew how huge the potential was and is: To this day, everyone I know who practices real estate investing (including me) touches only a tiny fraction of the total marketplace.

The second suggestion made even more powerful sense. I knew, from the various interviews I had done on radio and television, that time constraints and interviewers' lack of familiarity with what we were talking about might well misrepresent my message. Often, I was frustrated because just as I was warming to the subject, my allotted time was up. The Professional Education Institute proposed giving me an entire half-hour, uninterrupted by outside commercials. In that period of time, I could explain what real estate investing could promise to the typical individual.

The Institute wanted to know: Did I know anyone who had used my techniques and been successful as a real estate investor?

Did I ever!

Once I had a formal course ready, we put together a program and ran it on various television and cable stations. The interest was extraordinary.

Better yet: Those who bought my course began to write to us, telling what gigantic successes they had had. They represented the broadest spectrum of society — successful businesspeople, unsuccessful and out-of-work individuals, retirees, students, couples who wanted extra income, persons who were "looking for something to do," people who were handy with tools but didn't have a lot of money, casual investors — *everybody*. One after another, they wrote and phoned and sent photographs of the properties they had

First, let me say, THANK YOU. Because of your course I was able to buy a home with NO MONEY DOWN and receive a check at closing for $52,000. WOW . . . that was great.

I must tell you, at first I was a little unsure of this method of buying real estate with no money down.

When I received the course, I was ready to make my fortune.

When the course came I opened it and started to listen to the information on the tapes. I was motivated, but then got distracted, so I packed the course away. A few years later I lost my job, and one day as I was looking for my resume I came across the course in my closet. I started listening to the tapes again.

This time I went through the whole course and purchased my first home with no money down about two weeks later.

At closing I received a check for $52,000.00 and I now am selling the house for another $50,000.00 profit, for a total of $102,000.00, in six months. I could not have done this without your help.

— *Charles E. Jones, New York*

I know my story sounds unbelievable — I know this. But I swear it's true. I'm 26 years old, and when I got your course I was making $7,000 a year traveling as a musician in a band. I never finished college.

In the last year, I've bought 34 duplexes, 17 town homes, a 6-plex, and a lake house. My first deal was for 20 duplexes from one investor who was ready to get out. I must say, I let your course sit for a year prior to using it, then finally realized I had to do something. So, I got started. I found partners for some, and have put all of them on 15-year mortgages. Now, I know that when I'm 41, my positive cash flow will be $360,000 per year. My family's financial future is taken care of. I thank you for taking the time to share your knowledge. I know of very few people who would lay out for others all they know about how they became successful.

— *Dave Mulkey, Georgia*

bought as the result of taking the course. Some of their letters are reproduced in this book. You can see why I get so excited learning about their successes.

I'll answer Dave Mulkey's letter, belatedly, right here:

Dave, don't thank me. Thank yourself. I gave you the bat. You hit the ball out of the park. I gave you the cloth. You tailored it into a fine suit. I gave you the dictionary. You wrote the poem. I gave you the method. You proved it for yourself.

I admire people like Dave Mulkey. They work to improve their own futures. They don't quit. They study, then apply. They deserve success.

SUCCESS BREEDS SUCCESS

My television show was an instant hit. I like to think it was because what I was proposing was not only possible, it was probable. Those who bought my course found (sometimes to their surprise) that it worked.

Meanwhile, I myself continued to function as a real estate investor. I didn't want to be one of those "theoreticians" who preach but never practice.

Recognition has been wonderful frosting on the cake. I have been awarded the S.R.S. (Specialist in Real Estate Securities) designation by the Real Estate Securities and Syndication Institute. I've been listed in both *Who's Who in Real Estate* and *Who's Who in Real Estate in America.* In 1992 I was inducted into the Real Estate Investors' Hall of Fame. I've been invited to Washington twice to discuss real estate investing and the rights of property owners with key Congressional members. I've been on the covers of magazines such as *Income Plus, Income Opportunities, Opportunity World, Home Business Connection,* and *Oppportunity Maga-*

zine. And I've written a batch of books . . . including this one, which I regard as one of my most important works.

Along with my basic course, *How to Buy Your First Home or Investment Property with No Down Payment* (hefty title, isn't it?), I've prepared other audiocassette courses — *Cashing in on Foreclosures and Distress Properties — A Step by Step Formula, The Painless Guide to Profitable Property Management,* and *Creating Quick Wealth with Partners.* I also have videos, guides, and all kinds of materials ranging from *The Real Estate Computer Toolkit* to *The Investor's Edge Video Library.* I even have an advanced course, *The Real Estate Mastery Course.*

And I'm not only still going strong, I feel I'm just hitting my stride. The future for real estate investing is like the end of the rainbow: Nobody knows quite where it is, but everybody agrees: It's beautiful!

CHAPTER THREE

Jump-Starting Your Rocket to Wealth

*(Suggestion: Read this chapter **twice** before advancing to the next chapter. Let the message of this chapter flavor your attitude as you move along the financial highway to the wealth that can be yours.)*

COME ON IN, THE WATER'S FINE.

Enough about me.

Your turn.

You didn't buy this book to read the story of Carleton Sheets. The reason I opened up my personal background to you wasn't to have you applaud; no, it was to have you realize that you don't have to be born a millionaire to be a millionaire . . . and to get you to believe — even believe 1 percent — that you can do what I did.

I'll give you more proof than you've ever seen for any claim of success: That proof is absolute, unsolicited, solidly truthful testimony by *hundreds* of people who had no more background than you have (and maybe a lot less) and who, by following the principles I'm about to disclose, wound up working the system, creating an incredible extra income, amassing a huge net worth, and totally enjoying themselves. They're having the time of their lives making money, and there's no end in sight.

I am a single 55-year-old woman who was used to spending 60 hours every week on my poor, aching feet, selling in a retail store. No more! I bought your course the first time I saw you on television, and within six months I owned 23 units. Those 23 units give me $41,472 of annual income. I've completely replaced the income from my job, and my real estate work week is *well* less than ⅓ the hours!

I have no fears of retirement. I love life again! I feel good about providing nice housing to nice people. (I also rewarded myself by buying a red Grand Prix and a great time share — I'm going to New Orleans and Cancun!)

— *Carol Smith, Pennsylvania*

So if you bought this book because you have even a 1 percent belief that you can make a ton of money, I'm out to up that 1 percent to 100 percent. And if you've already heard about me and my course and already believe my system works, I'm about to make you happy . . . because, yes, it does work.

A mild disclaimer:

We live in strange times. The work ethic is kind of rare these days. People want to go to sleep one night and awake the next morning able to speak Hungarian. If you're one of those, somebody who wants something for nothing, somebody who keeps saying, "The world owes me a living" — and then wonders why their lifestyle always moves sideways, from near-miss to near-miss — well then, I fear my words aren't for you.

Those who have finished my course and applied the principles are as different from "The world owes me a living" person as the ant is from the grasshopper. They think like winners, not losers. And the results prove them right!

So right off the bat, let's please agree on two basic "Rules of the Road":

Rule 1: You're your own boss. That's the wonder of it all! Nobody else is telling you what to do — *you* are telling *you* what to do. That means if you *don't* tell *you* what to do, you'll flounder and give up. Lots of people like that are around. There are lots of losers around.

But please, please recognize your own state of mind: *You bought this book. You're thinking like a winner.* That's half the deal right there, don't you agree?

Rule 2: By the time you've absorbed the message in this book, you'll have a minimum of a 1000 percent edge over 99.9 percent of the populace. That's *minimum*. Maximum? You'll know more about making money in real estate than most professional real estate agents. You'll quickly — and I mean *quickly* — be buying property. You may buy a home for yourself, a far bigger and more luxurious home than you thought you would ever be able to own for years to come, with no money down and with great terms. You may buy a dozen rental homes, and even some business property, wheeling and dealing and making tens of thousands of dollars with your new negotiating skills.

It's all there. And it's all up to you.

Now, here's the frosting on the cake: It's simple.

"WILL IT WORK FOR ME?"

This book is *not* fiction. I can answer, unequivocally: Yes! You can apply the principles right away. Yes! You can buy property with no money down right away. Yes! You can do this even if you have no credit or even if you have *negative* credit.

Do you think real estate investing works only in major metropolitan markets? No! If you want to operate in a small town, I have a happy surprise for you:

The techniques you'll discover in this book will work just as well in a small town as they will in a big city. The need for action in selling or buying a home doesn't change and the circumstances don't change. It doesn't depend on the population of any area. In some ways — for example, advertising — a smaller community has advantages bigger markets don't have, because the marketplace is more compact. Big city, small town? No difference. What matters is big *thinking*, which will outpull small thinking every time.

Are you interested in business property (or buying a business) as well as residential property . . . or instead of residential property? It doesn't matter!

The techniques described in this book work. They work for *any* kind of property, because they're logical, they're practical, and they fill a definite niche in the real estate industry. For that matter, they'll work for any buy/sell situation — diamonds, surplus merchandise, automobiles. But those aren't the purpose of this book. Real estate promises the greatest reward. Real estate can make you a millionaire, as it has so many others. In vernacular lingo, real estate is where it's at! Oh, there are a lot of books written and a lot of shows on television that "hype" the opportunities that exist for a person going into business for

I'm 43 years old, happily married, and have two boys at home, one in college. I'm also a full-time investor now. I used to be in corporate America, which required lots of time away from home. Now, I feel very fortunate and blessed . . . not only because of the freedoms that our real estate gives us financially (a $78,000 a year income and over $640,000 of net worth) but because of the peace of mind that we are debt free, we live independently, give generously to charity, and are living a life long dream.

— *J.E. Parrott, Virginia*

him or herself . . . everything from selling excess and discontinued merchandise by running classified ads, to running a 900 telephone number — business is touted as a way to make some big money. But let's face it. No business in the world can compare with owning an asset, like rental real estate, that other people (tenants) are buying for you. Again, real estate is where it's at.

HOW TO AVOID POTHOLES ON YOUR ROAD TO RICHES

You don't look at someone and ask, "Why aren't you rich?" Too many variables enter into the mixture, but the biggest variable is the individual's own attitude toward life and success.

You *should* look at yourself in the mirror and ask, "Why aren't you rich?" If you're totally honest with yourself, the answer might be, "Because I don't have the confidence to take those steps that would make me rich." Or, "I don't know how to do it."

My suggestion is that right now, with this book in your hands, you walk over to the mirror, look yourself in the eye, and proclaim: "I have the knowledge right here in my hand, and I'm going to use it and get rich!"

Carleton, we bought your course in March. You would not believe the success we've had in just 5 months! We now own 16 units — we've increased our net worth $757,000, and make about $2,800 a month in spendable cash. The best part is that everything we've done, we've done with no money down.

We don't have to worry about education costs for our 4 children, and a vacation every year is in the budget. We're dreaming bigger, and our goals are bigger. We're even building our dream home right now! We never realized that investing could be so fun! Thank you!
— *Andy and Donna Quargnenti, Missouri*

"BUT I DON'T KNOW ANYTHING ABOUT REAL ESTATE"

Hey, we aren't talking about brain surgery here.

Or, maybe we are . . . because if you reject the logic you're about to encounter in these pages with the statement, "But I don't know anything about real estate," your first move is to perform a little brain surgery on yourself: Cut out those negative brain cells and throw them away.

In fact, of every 100 people who have studied my course, 85 to 90 have absolutely no background in real estate. None. Zero. Does that get in the way of their success? Certainly not, because while no one would argue that background is usually helpful, what you're about to read is specifically tailored for those who *don't* have a background in real estate. In fact, professional real estate agents and brokers should be working for you, saving you legwork. So please, forget that excuse because it simply doesn't exist.

Does that mean there's a great deal to learn before you can launch your real estate investment business? You don't have to memorize the techniques; all you have to do is start using them, using this book (or the audios or videos in my system, if you are one who learns better that way) as a reference.

We're dealing in logic, not technical details. That's why you don't need a real estate license. You don't need a big bank account. You don't even need a down payment. You only need an understanding of the logical steps, the strategies, and the techniques and the willingness to dip a toe in waters that can be remarkably warm and profitable.

Ever try to sell your home without a real estate broker? Tough, isn't it? That may be why some folks make the statement, "But I don't know anything about real estate."

Well, it *isn't* tough. If you have a home and are considering selling it, please study this book before trying to market it. I promise: You'll be exposed to *dozens* of tips and procedures that will make the sale of your home easier, faster, and more profitable. It's a matter of turning the creative buying techniques around 180 degrees, putting on your seller's hat, and taking action.

The "counter-statement" (which is *also* incorrect) to "But I don't know anything about real estate" is, "Aha! Just buy any property you can get for no money down. That's all there is to it."

I suspect you wouldn't have bought this book if you'd had that attitude — a combination of wishful thinking and disbelief. Oh, I've met people like that. They may listen to me for 15 minutes, or, for that matter, read just this far in this text, and say, "The rest is all window-trimming. Let's go find some property for no money down."

So they scour the classified ads in the newspaper and look for flexible sellers. Here's one that says, "Highly motivated." Here's another one that says, "Must sell this weekend." And off they go, making an offer. Without knowing *how* to buy with no money down, they can face hidden problems that can haunt them for months or even years — problems such as negative cash flow, or bad terms, or balloon payments, or management problems, or tenants who tear the property to pieces. Or they just plain pay too much for the property. Let me make an emphatic statement: Profits are made in real estate when you buy, not when you sell.

Or they'll ignore the biggest problem of all: "No money down" has to be explained to the seller so the seller sees benefits. And there are benefits for the seller, but obviously only if *you* know what they are and how to present them.

Before we're done you'll have the answers to all of those problems. They aren't difficult, but they aren't obvious either.

The logic is as simple as this: If you were building a home, you wouldn't say, "Aha! All I need is a hammer and some lumber." If you're buying a home, "No money down" is an operating philosophy, not the be-all-end-all.

"BUT THE BROKER SAYS . . ."

I'll keep saying throughout this book: Brokers work for us. Actually, it's better if brokers work *with* us. They can save us a lot of legwork in exchange for commissions to which they're certainly entitled.

> When I bought the course, just paying for it was hard. But in less than 6 months, I made over $33,000 cash profit with real estate. I'd have to work 3 years as a nurse to make what I made with your course.
>
> I've got real estate agents coming to me and asking how am I doing this. I tell them, "Order the course and you'll find out how I'm doing this."
>
> — *Lynn Self, Virginia*

You don't need a broker if you can approach an owner directly. If you can't, hook up with a good broker or agent.

And here's a key I hope you won't forget: Go with the broker when he or she presents your offer. Before you say, "Huh?" or "But the broker won't let me," follow the logic. You eventually, and maybe immediately, will encounter a situation in which you want to make a no money down offer. The broker not only might try to discourage you — "At least include a five thousand dollar down payment" — but also might present your offer in a negative way. The undecided seller is swayed by the broker's lack of enthusiasm or being told, "You might want to wait until you get an offer accompanied by some cash."

If you go with that broker, you're assured of a positive presentation. Now, to be sure you're free to accompany the broker or agent. I include in all my offers (along with a whole slew of other clauses designed to protect us buyers) that I (or you, the buyer) reserve the right to accompany the broker when presenting the offer. Easy, isn't it?

As I'll mention later, I've spent over 25 years and paid thousands of dollars in legal fees to develop an offer form that appears standard and that protects the buyer — not the broker or seller.

When your offer includes this clause, the broker may say it's unprofessional. The broker may say he or she doesn't work that way. The broker may say your being there will kill the chance of a sale. The broker may say if you're there the seller won't be inclined to negotiate. The broker may say the seller doesn't want you there. The broker may, in fact, become abusive, telling you that you don't know how real estate deals are handled.

Whatever that broker says, you have a quick and gentle reminder: The law says the broker can't deny you the right to be there.

So okay, *why* do you want to be there? Because once you're there, you can explain to the seller that the broker was kind enough to let you explain the offer in person. You can then explain the benefits to both seller and buyer — benefits that will be made clear as this text progresses.

A quick preliminary tip: Arrive at the appointed time, separately. Don't come in the broker's car, because you want to leave before the broker does. When you've finished explaining your offer, *don't* pull the typical salesperson stunt of asking, "Well, what do you think?" or, "How does that sound to you?" If you come off as a salesperson, all the logic washes away in the sea of distrust people naturally have for those who are obviously "pitching."

Instead, tell the seller you know he or she or they will want to discuss your offer with the broker, and that they should feel free to call you if they have a question. Give them your card. Then leave. By the way, if it's an out-of-town seller, ask to present the offer by telephone with the broker in a conference call.

You'll find, if you use this method, that the possibility of getting a positive counter-offer goes up 100 percent.

"HOW MUCH OF MY TIME IS THIS GOING TO TAKE?"

The great majority of those who decide to follow my lead and begin enjoying the profits of real estate investing have other fish to fry.

Some are students. Many have full-time jobs. Some are homemakers. Some are retired or semi-retired. Some are business executives. Some are, at their moment of decision, down on their luck, taking what they believe may be their last chance for success. And, believe it or not, some are in the real estate business.

You can see that it's the broadest possible spectrum. My students absolutely represent a cross-section of society.

We currently own three businesses in West Virginia. Now, in only nine months since studying your course, our real estate already gives us over half of the income our businesses do. (Our real estate gives us over $60,000 per year of income.)

We have three kids in college and after it provides for our retirement, we'll pass these properties on to them. All the while, they'll learn how to invest so they too can choose whether to work for themselves or for someone else.

All of our rental units were purchased no money down, and in fact, we got cash back at closing on most. We think anyone who's in their 40s like we are, or any age, should consider how quickly real estate can provide them with a nice supplemental income and retirement plan.

— *Bill and Nancy Fugman, West Virginia*

And the wonderful part of it all is that success stories abound, within every group.

The most commonly asked question, as an individual or couple begins learning about my system through my books and tapes, is, "I don't have a lot of time to devote to this. How much time will it take me to buy a piece of property?"

I'll give you a ballpark answer: After you've absorbed the information that underlies the system, you should be able to buy that first piece of property in about six weeks, allocating a few hours a week in your spare time to the quest (not much, out of a 168-hour week). Some have even told me they've gone out and made a profitable deal the very first *day!* . . . but don't count on it, although if it happens, fine.

That's for *one* piece of property. And, yes, that's where some do stop. They just want to own a home or have a single investment property, and they buy it with no money down. Good for them. They have what they've wanted.

But, if you're looking to build a net worth up into seven figures by being a serious real estate investor, buying and selling real estate on an increasingly professional level, you'd better count on committing five to 10 hours a week. Real estate investing parallels any other profession. The more time you give it, the bigger the results are likely to be. So 10 hours a week will bring you greater response — and greater wealth — than five hours a week. And 40 hours a week, a full-time job, should pay off substantially better than a mere 10 hours a week. The trick is that the more you do it, the better you get, and you accomplish more in less time. Many of my students are full time investors because they can't afford not to be.

The arithmetic is simple. But, what you *don't* want to do is start off with a flurry and then let your activity taper down. That's what the amateurs do. To avoid that deadly taper-down effect, I suggest you buy a one-year diary and record the amount of time you spend on real estate invest-

Since I bought your course 1½ years ago, my life has changed tremendously. Before that, for 27 years I was a contractor, getting paid only nine months a year, getting up early, working late (always on somebody **else's** schedule), and in a very physically demanding and stressful job.

I'm now a full time investor. My income is over $60,000 a year and growing. I have what I consider to be an "automatic investment plan" because each year I have more and more equity in my property, and the value is going up. My net worth after 1½ years of investing is $460,000. It was nowhere near that — nowhere — after 27 years as a contractor. I have less stress, my income is steady year round, and I spend more time relaxing with my family.

I commend you for putting together a common sense, step-by-step course. Thank you.

— Joseph Vousden, New York

ing each day or each week, in the diary. (Franklin Covey has a day planner which really fits the needs of a real estate investor.) Be honest with yourself because you're both the boss and the employee. If you see yourself tapering down, make a conscious effort to pick up the tempo.

Person after person has reported a gradual *increase* in the number of hours devoted to real estate investing, until this becomes their primary job — their primary source of

> I've been in real estate now only about 18 months since I got your course. It's amazing what kind of a part-time income you can build up in rents. After all my mortgage payments and expenses, my properties give me $72,000 a year. That's in my spare time!
>
> I use most of the money to invest in more real estate. I had never bought property before — didn't know a thing about real estate. Now, I look forward to every day. The course is phenomenal — my life wouldn't be the same without it.
>
> — *John Azar, North Carolina*

income. And no wonder, because these people are making far more money, hour for hour, than they ever have in their lives. Not only that, they're having a good time and are becoming important people in their community.

The key word on which every successful real estate investor agrees: Commitment. The first commitment is to complete this book and then, if you are really serious, my home study course. The next commitment is to spend a specific amount of spare time buying real estate, but in a proper and safe way. The third commitment is to ignore failures and concentrate on successes. Do you think someone who makes half a dozen phone calls and hasn't yet found a property owner willing to negotiate, and then gets discouraged and quits, has shown any commitment? I don't.

As you read these words, you're in a specific financial posture. Obviously, I can't begin to guess whether you're rich or poor. But I'll certainly guess that you're not 100 percent satisfied with where you are. That's not only good, it's excellent, because it tells me you want more than you have now. That's the perfect beginning for making a lot of money as a real estate investor. And I commend you for making the right choice. I know it comes as no surprise to you to learn that all people are where they are, rich or poor, because of choices they make in life.

LET ME MAKE SOMETHING ABSOLUTELY CLEAR

Many, many people who have heard of my system, but haven't penetrated it and don't really know how it works, think it's like the old cliché about the stock market: Buy low, sell high. For example, if a home with a fair market value of $600,000 can be bought for say, $400,000, they think it's a good deal to be snapped up. By the time you've finished this book you'll know better. Trying to get a decent cash flow with rental income from a home in that stratosphere is really difficult. Also, a home that expensive is not easy to "flip." Not only ease of turnover, but *safety*, results from buying "bread and butter" houses that the average working family will live in. That's what will create wealth for you, with a minimum of risk.

Some of the "Doubting Thomases" (and some who just run scared) ask, "What happens if real estate goes down in value?" Let's get basic. When you buy a piece of property you can expect one of three results:

A. It will go up in value.
B. It will remain the same in value.
C. It will go down in value.
    (I told you it would be basic.)

All right, let's examine all three possibilities. For the last century and a half property has gone up in value. So the odds are with you. And keep in mind, I'm not telling you to go and buy just *any* property and *hope* that it goes up in value. I'll show you how to pick the right kinds of properties, and then how to actively manage your properties so that you cause them to increase in value.

If the property stays the same and doesn't go up in value, you're still ahead because of tax benefits, cash flow, and the equity you're building up as the mortgage is paid down, so it's a good investment in that event as well. Your tenants are buying your properties for you.

The possibility does exist that an individual property might decrease in value. But you can't be badly damaged because you can't lose more than you've invested in the property . . . and if you buy it my way, with little or no money down, you have little or no risk. Again, the tenants have been paying for it all along, through their payments of rent.

Unlike the stock market or money speculation, my techniques don't depend on inflation to make money for you. We're dealing in methods and procedures I've tested, proved, and refined for almost 30 years, and a lot of people have said, "Thank you for teaching us how to make money day after day, month after month, year after year."

Before we get into the real meat of this book and the re-markable profits you have every right to expect, I want to answer loudly and clearly the question some nay-sayers

> I've been a college professor for 13 years, and I can think of no better way for people to earn a living than real estate. Our net spendable income from rentals, af-ter expenses, is over $208,000 per year. We're now build-ing our dream home and I've never been happier at my job than now (now that I don't have to work, it's fun!). Your course is easy for anyone to understand and the freedom people can achieve is tremendous.
> — *David Henneberry, Oklahoma*

will raise. That question is, "If you offer to give a seller a promissory note (an I.O.U.) instead of actual cash, isn't it true the seller will walk away from the offer?"

No, it isn't true, and once again we have many thousands of transactions to prove it. Do all sellers need cash? Absolutely not. Oh, some sellers do, but by no means all. And if the seller does need cash, you can show him or her how to convert your note into cash. (That's one reason you want to accompany a broker if the broker is presenting your offer.) It's fine for the seller to get cash — as long as it isn't yours.

Here's the logic behind your no money down offer making sense to a seller when an actual cash offer might not make sense:

We all know how to generate hostility in a seller — by offering a "lowball" price the seller may think is insulting. That's the kind of negotiation two warring nations enter into at a "peace" conference where they hate each other going in. And that's what so many real estate transactions become, including those in which a broker represents both parties.

Now, compare that with one of the approaches you might use: You let the seller name the price. You name the terms. It's a win/win situation in which everybody gets something and doesn't feel exploited. You're giving the seller the asking price and merely hammering out the means of payment. You become a problem-solver. You buy the property. And again, as you will see later, the seller can still leave the closing table with cash in his or her pocket.

What's the difference, after all, between you and all those others who let their lack of confidence and lack of drive keep them buried in the same economic position for most of their lives? I can answer that question in one sentence: You bought this book and they didn't.

That may be a simplistic answer, because buying the book is Step One, and I know from experience how many people take that first step and then stop. Their defeatist attitude isn't limited to real estate; it permeates their lives. I've become convinced that 95 percent of the people in the United States work just hard enough to avoid getting fired. And, to be fair, I should add — they're probably paid just enough to keep them from quitting.

You know many people like this. They come home from work or school and sit down in front of the television set. They watch shows that depict great wealth. And they dream a little — "Boy, I wish I had that kind of money. Boy, I wish I were rich" — but dreams are *not* powerful enough to amass great wealth. That's not how it happens.

It happens from consistent alertness, from consistent determination, from a consistent stick-to-it attitude, from consistent action, from consistent refusal to succumb to the 95 percent defeatist outlook that can come up with 95 different reasons why real estate investing won't work. And it comes from the right knowledge.

Well, guess what? It works! It has worked for others and it will work for you. Be grateful that you are not one of the 95 percent of the people who are on the other side, growing old without money, the worst disease in the world.

The universal language of the poor is "I'll do it tomorrow." No. Do it today. Use that diary I spoke of earlier. Stay in command and success will follow.

Are you a renter? The difference is that if you've been renting for some years you probably have paid for your own home several times over and have nothing to show for it. You'll see, in these very pages, how to buy your own home with little or no money down, perhaps with monthly payments less than your current rent payments!

I think of one woman who has been living in an apartment, in one of the buildings I own, for 17 years. Her rent when she moved in was $270. But I've been nice. I've only raised it to $490. Still, she has paid $87,000 in rent, almost three times what the unit cost.

In another case, I knew a couple in New Hampshire who had lived in the same unit for 52 years. It was a two-story home. But after their children were grown and left home, the owner was "nice" enough to let them occupy the lower floor only. He then added a kitchen and rented the upstairs to another tenant. Smart landlord. Dumb tenants.

> Carleton, I'm 70 years old. I was a minister for over 50 years. We just enjoyed our 50th wedding anniversary. Can you imagine our feelings when I retired? I had no house, no job, no money, no medical insurance, and a retirement of about $400 per month from the church.
>
> Thank the Lord for real estate and your instruction. All my real estate (we have 24 units now) we bought with no money down. Our income is over $3,000 a month — whether we work or not — and we have easy living. We're encouraging our four kids to get started now.
>
> — *Rev. Kenneth and Ida Williams, Oklahoma*

Are you recently divorced or widowed? If so, start building your credit (see chapter 5) and you'll have a whole new positive perspective.

Do you need money for education, whether for yourself or your children? Do you need money to travel? Do you need money for a new car or a new wardrobe or a new start? Would you like to help out your local church or help a friend or family member in need? Get it through real estate.

So that's the basic story. Excited? I hope so, because *it does work.* You literally have in your hands the tools and weapons to make it work. You can reap the rewards that are due to those who apply themselves and use tested principles.

My final imperative for this chapter: Don't wait! Get started now! Thinking "tomorrow" puts you with the stifled 95 percent. Thinking today means you're on your way *right now.*

Come on in. The water's fine!

CHAPTER FOUR

How to Create Wealth Out of Thin Air

*(Suggestion: More important than technical knowledge is confidence in your own abilities. As you absorb the information in this chapter, relate it to yourself. **You** can do what so many others have done! **You** can become financially independent, starting with little or no investment! Only you can know if my emphatic pronouncements apply to you, but I think they do. Why? Because others have proved there's no magic involved. Success is as simple and direct as willingness to follow the procedures set forth in this book.)*

SHAZAM!

Remember the comic book hero of the 1930s and 1940s, Captain Marvel?

He was just a youngster named Billy Batson. But when he shouted the magic word "Shazam!" . . . well, things happened. He became Captain Marvel, who could do just about anything.

Now, why am I reminding you about Captain Marvel?

It's because in this chapter I'm about to show you how you can be a Captain Marvel of making money, real money, with real estate. All you have to do is understand — and use — the principles of wealth creation.

Here is where the real decision-making process either hardens out of the pages of this book or turns to water. I can show you what to do. I can (and will) show you what others have done. What I can't do is shout "Shazam!" for you. *You* have to be your own Captain Marvel. *You* are the one who has to say, "Yes, this will work for me. I've seen the proof and now it's *my* turn to cash in on it." *You* are the transforming agent, the bow *and* arrow, the decision-maker.

It's as simple as this:

Suppose a friend serves you the most delicious cake you've ever tasted. You say to the friend, "Gee, I wish I could have cake like that once a week."

Your friend says, "Of course you can have cake like this every week. Here is the recipe."

You know what? Some people would quit right there. They'd say to themselves, "If this were a real friend, she wouldn't just give me the recipe. She'd bake a cake for me every week."

That's how those who lose out on so much of what life has to offer — that's how they think.

Winners are grateful for the recipe. Suddenly *they* have a capability they never had before — the capability of baking an unusually delicious cake. They take that recipe, and every week they enjoy fresh, wonderful cake, often experimenting, adding their own unique ingredients . . . while their neighbor, waiting for somebody else to bake the cake for him, just sits there brooding and wondering when he'll ever get another slice of cake.

Usually, that neighbor never eats another slice of cake. That neighbor doesn't cause things to happen; no, he waits for something to happen. Yes, my friend, that's how not to think.

All right. Time to shout "Shazam!" Time to understand and start using the tools and weapons that are right there in your own mental cupboard. Time to start transforming Billy Batson into Captain Marvel.

We want to share some of the success we've enjoyed since my wife and daughter gave me your course as a Christmas present . . .

We bought our $250,000 home with no money down. We didn't do a lease option; rather we found a motivated builder who accepted our "nice" $100,000 home as a partial trade-in; and gave us a $22,000 allowance for landscaping. We actually walked out of closing with a check for $900. We have since moved out of that home.

Photograph A is a view of the Atlantic Ocean from the deck of our condominium which we now occupy. Not only did we buy it with no money down; but we left closing with about $5,100 in our pocket. We're now occupying it as our primary home; and renting the adjacent units, which we already own. By the way, we bought both, as well, with no money down.

Photograph A

Photograph B is of a V.A. owned home which we bought in February, again with no money down . . . We're enjoying an $117.00 per month positive cash flow, after paying all expenses.

In fact, we've developed, and are adhering to a business plan which has allowed us to give up our day jobs; relocate; and live the life of full time real estate investors.

We have your course to thank for that . . .

Where are we now? We've got a net worth of over $1 million. Our rentals generate a monthly cash flow of $6,400. We'll close on our next property in two weeks.

We're enjoying an ocean front condominium. We're able to enjoy some of the physical rewards of our efforts, a new Mercedes and matching Rolex watches just to name two. We don't have to worry about Jackie's college tuition; and we didn't have to hesitate in approving an upcoming trip to Australia, despite the hefty fees . . .

Photograph B

So far, we've acquired 21 properties; have one in escrow (about to be closed upon).

The opportunities are out there. One needs merely to recognize them; develop a plan; and be bold enough to grab hold.

— *Tom and Janet Srock, North Carolina*

I contacted Tom about a year after he and Janet wrote this letter, and he reported that they had increased their holdings to 29 properties. I congratulated him.

You know what Tom Srock said? "I can honestly say it's easier to buy a piece of property than it is to buy a suit."

Ready to say "Shazam!" as Tom and Janet Srock did? Then let's go!

CAN YOU *EVER* "SAVE" YOUR WAY TO A BIG NET WORTH?

Set yourself a timetable. It will prevent you from drifting. It also gives you a "handle" for judging your progress.

I've had many hundreds of people who took my course — the same course referred to in this book — tell me, casually, that their timetable called for an increase of their net worth of $1 million to $2 million over the next two years . . . or $2 million to $5 million. These are the same people who would have gasped a few years earlier, if I had suggested to them that they'd have a net worth anywhere near $1 million.

I don't have a "crystal ball." I only furnish the knowledge of how to make the money. They are the ones who control their individual destinies, just as you control yours.

Question: Can you imagine trying to *save* your way to a $1 million net worth? Even if you could save $10,000 a year, and achieve a 10 percent return on your money, it would take about 25 years. For the average hard-working individual, it's just not possible. Saving is a good idea. I believe in it; but in no way can saving compete with the big rewards possible in real estate investing.

No other investment can even come close to real estate in the huge benefits this endeavor makes possible. Certainly no other investment has so great a potential for creating wealth out of thin air.

Do you wonder why, if this is true, everybody doesn't pile into real estate? Sure, I've wondered too. But I think I know the answer. The reason has to be that most people either aren't aware of this opportunity; or, if they are aware, because of having seen me on TV or for some other reason, they don't know how to take advantage of it. Or, they're waiting for me or someone else to bake the cake!

One deterrent is mind-set. People are literally programmed to think if they don't have a lot of money, they can't buy property.

By the time you've finished this book, you will, I hope, decide to spend five to seven hours a week making money in real estate, creating wealth out of thin air. That's *you*. Most people would rather spend those five to seven hours watching television.

So much the better for us!

The federal government estimates that 92 percent of the adult population will be dependent on the government in order to have any kind of lifestyle after age 65. Only one percent can be considered wealthy. One percent!

Look at the supermarkets. Look at the fast food restaurants. Count the number of senior citizens who have to work part-time in order to live with even a minimum amount of comfort.

Think of your friends and neighbors. Which of them will have the affluence we all dream about? The answer you should come up with is *you*, because once you've reasonably mastered the principles of real estate investing, your net worth can increase in giant steps.

THE FOUR KEYS TO WEALTH OUT OF THIN AIR:

You might decide to list investments that can increase your wealth without your having to work day and night.

Stocks come to mind at once. Mutual funds and bonds are less explosive. Historically, the stock market has yielded investors approximately 10 percent per year on their money. But, talk about volatility! You can lose 30 percent to 50 percent of your money in one year. Regardless, that 10 percent per year average profit on stocks looks pretty small compared with what we can make on our real estate investments, as you will soon see. Some people invest in gold and silver, because they always have worth; but during the last 15 years, the value of such an investment actually went down significantly. Speculators invest in motion pictures and stage-plays; they can claim glamor, but they have *zero* control over their investment.

Rare coins and collectibles are popular "investments" for some people. They're long-range, and certainly no investor in these items can claim that they represent short-term profits.

What do all those investments have in common? They all are risky, and they all require that you have money to get started!

So what *should* the ideal investment include for you?

- ✔ income
- ✔ growth
- ✔ tax advantages
- ✔ leverage

Let's examine these, in order:

Income:

Income means what it implies: Your investment generates money that you can spend each month.

No other investment can consistently provide as much income, based on the amount of money invested, as real estate.

Later in these pages we'll explore the technique of creating a financial analysis of property; but right now, understand clearly: When you have rental income coming in on your property, you have certain expenses connected with owning that property. You also have a mortgage payment. Whatever is left is that marvelous term: *cash flow.*

Well, it's marvelous if we add one qualifier: *positive* cash flow.

Real estate can generate a remarkable positive cash flow. I'll give you a personal example:

I bought a single-family home for $60,000. The rental income is $650. The expenses (maintenance, management, taxes, insurance, mortgage payments, etc.) are $523. It has a positive cash flow of $127 a month. So from this one investment, without having to do much except keep my eye on it, I'm banking about $1,500 a year. The previous owner, who sold me the property, received $5,800 cash when we closed on it. That $5,800 cash didn't come from my bank account. I bought the property for no money down.

Here's how I did it. The seller took back a wraparound mortgage for $54,200 and agreed to pay all the closing costs because I paid the full asking price for his property. The source for the $5,800 was as follows: $650 rent from the tenant for my first month of ownership; a credit from the seller for $1,150 for a security deposit of $500 and a last month's rent of $650, which the tenant had paid earlier; a short-term 12 month note for $2,000 to the seller at zero interest; and the balance of $2,000 as an advance against one of my credit cards.

Do I have to pay the $4,000 back? Sure, but with $1,500 a year coming in from the property which I had purchased with no cash from my pocket, how tough was it? In truth, with that particular property, the cash flow had increased to $155 a month by the third year, my equity build-up (mortgage pay-down) was over $1,000 during the first three years, the tax loss I was able to use to offset other income amounted to over $6,000 during the first three years (resulting in actual tax savings of approximately $1,500), and finally, despite paying the seller's asking price, the property had risen in value to nearly $70,000 by the end of the third year. I still own the property after 14 years. It's been a gold mine.

Okay, but suppose I'd had to write a check for $5,800. Would that have been so terrible? I'd be out $5,800; but in exchange I'd get $1,500 a year, and that's a 26 percent return. Not bad! (A person buying a stock would be delighted to get a 26 percent return in one year; and that person would be ecstatic to be able to count on that return year after year.)

But getting the $1,500 a year *without* laying out the $5,800 is much better. As a real estate investor, you'll soon take for granted the kind of rates of returns that stock market investors can only dream of.

Growth:

Here's a flat statement I challenge anyone to refute: *Real estate is going to rise in value.*

Yes, that's a broad and all-encompassing statement. Yes, we have occasional dips in real estate on a regional basis and sometimes (though very infrequently) on a national basis. But these are relatively tiny and temporary. Real estate, as an investment, has gone up *steadily* over the past 165 years.

(It's actually much longer than that, but records only go back that far. Do you remember reading that the Indians sold Manhattan for $24 worth of trinkets?)

Even in the past 15 years (as of press time), real estate has gone up at a compounded rate approaching 5 percent. And I'll tell you where some of the best opportunities for investors like us will be: those occasional narrow pockets where real estate is having a temporary retrenchment. We take advantage of it. In fact, even if the value goes down after you've bought property, you aren't hurt unless you sell right then. Your positive cash flow continues. Smart investors hold property until the time is right. Sometimes, the right time to sell is immediately after you buy . . . or even *before* you buy.

(Some of the more aggressive individuals who have taken my home study course have bought not only houses and business property but real estate companies as well.)

You see, "growth" in real estate comes not only from appreciation, but also from equity buildup — courtesy of your tenants' rent payments. Early in my career, I heard a

It's been 25 months since I bought Carleton's course and things are going great. After creatively buying the local Century 21 Office I was able to buy the local Better Homes & Gardens Office the same way and bring the two offices together as one.

One real estate office purchase was only a $2,000 down payment; for the other, I got cash back at closing. The money is rolling in nicely.

— *Jimmy Smith,*
North Carolina

statement that I'll never forget: "Real estate is truly an asset that pays for itself."

Going back to the $60,000 house I bought, with 5 percent appreciation, my equity went up $3,000. If my mortgage was paid down by $1,000, that's a $4,000 equity gain. If I include the cash flow of approximately $1,500, now my gain is $5,500. Even if I had made a $5,800 down payment, I would have had almost a 100% return! The reality, though, is that I put zero down, so my annual return is infinite. Are you excited yet?

Tax advantages:

A fact: Most people work between four and five months each year just to pay their taxes. That's right. Most people work until early May for free!

That is: It takes about four to five months of your total income to pay all your state and federal income taxes and your social security taxes each year.

But if you're a real estate investor, it's actually possible to cut that tax liability by buying investment property. Every property you buy *reduces* the amount you owe the IRS at the end of the year!

So consider this: If you're able to save on taxes from an investment property . . . and that's aside from the money you're getting from your positive cash-flow . . . it's extra money in your pocket every month.

Possible? Not only possible; it's exactly what you can expect, because of the tax breaks you get (and deserve) as a real estate investor. In the case of the $60,000 property, tack on another $400 or so in actual tax savings in one year, and I'm up to almost $6,000 as a return on my investment. Now, remember, I *invested* nothing — and many of my students do this and actually get cash back when they buy property. You heard right. They buy a property no money down and leave the closing table with spendable cash.

Leverage:

"It takes money to make money."

We've all heard this since childhood. But SHAZAM! It doesn't have to be *your* money to make money. That's the whole premise of my course and this book: Use *other people's* money. The word for using other people's money is *leverage*.

You read in the newspapers and financial magazines every week about "leveraged buyouts," some of them in the billions of dollars. Do the investors who buy those giant corporations put up their own cash?

Sometimes they do, if they're rich enough. But oddly, the richer they are, the less likely they are to use their own money. The very rich know what you're about to know — the principles of leveraging. They operate the way I want you to operate — by leveraging. Leverage is the nucleus of creating wealth out of thin air.

And, you have an edge over every other type of leveraged deal. No other type of investment allows the type of leverage allowed in real estate.

The arithmetic is simple:

If you pay all cash for a piece of property, there's no leverage. If you put 10 percent down and borrow 90 percent, that's a 90 percent leveraged property. So if you put no money down and all the money comes from one or more other sources, that property is 100 percent leveraged.

Warning: It's possible to buy a property with no money down and wind up with a *negative* cash flow. So don't assume buying property with no money down is the be-all-end-all of creating wealth out of thin air. No money down is the *means*. Positive cash flow is the *end*. Don't ever let the means substitute for the end.

That's where financial analysis comes in. And just one rule applies:

Be honest.

With whom? With yourself. Your financial analysis will tell you, straight and simple, whether or not if you buy that property with no money down you'll have a positive cash flow. Don't be blinded by a "Wow, I didn't have to put up any cash!" attitude. A cool, dispassionate attitude not only can make you rich; it can make you very rich!

YOU HAVE *CONTROL!*

You can think all day and not come up with another type of investment that gives you the *control* you have when you're buying real estate.

You determine the terms of the purchase. *You* set the management policies. *You* decide how and when you're going to fix up the property or paint it or make cosmetic improvements . . . or do nothing at all. *You* determine whether you'll rent it furnished or unfurnished. *You* pick the tenants. You set the terms of how you'll be paid — weekly or semi-monthly or monthly. *You're* in control.

So don't think of this as a hobby (although it can take less time than some hobbies). You're running a business. Yes, it starts out as a small business, but it can grow faster than you'd ever imagine once you're in it. (Can you imagine what would happen to the young people in America if practical, how-to-do-it information like what is in my home study course were included in every college curriculum?)

Twelve months ago I purchased the course as a 21-year-old college senior. Today I own seven rental properties with almost $18,000 annual positive cash flow. Also, I have $210,000 in equity and have made about $7,000 cash from refinances. I plan to quit my job and be a full-time investor by the end of the year. THANK YOU, CARLETON SHEETS!

— *Adam M. Corder, Georgia*

Well, thank you, Adam. You're proving . . . as so many others have proved . . . that if you follow the system you can make a lot of money.

Best of all, real estate investing is fun. I mean it! I hear this wherever I go, when I have conversations with those who have moved into real estate investing my way: "It's the most fun I've ever had." Me, too!

And that's a point to consider: Don't take a deadly serious, life-or-death attitude toward negotiations. Say to yourself, "Negotiating is fun" . . . and mean it. You'll find not only that you'll close more deals, but you'll also find that every deal is easier to close than it will be if you take yourself too seriously. I'll have more to say about negotiaton later on and even give you a fool-proof checklist to work with.

Until you actually own property, you can't even guess at the pride of ownership you'll experience. It isn't like owning anything else in the world. You'll buy a new car and feel proud for the first couple of weeks. You'll buy an elegant new outfit and feel proud the first few times you wear it.

But property — every time you drive by, your heart will swell with pride: "I own that!" You'll bring your family to look at it. (Even after you've sold the place for a nice profit, you'll still feel pride when you see it.) You'll improve the neighborhood — which the neighborhood will appreciate. You'll be treated differently by professionals such as bankers, agents, and businesspeople who not only recognize you as an economic equal but also recognize you as a source of profitable business for themselves. Nothing equals the feeling of pride you experience when you own real estate.

INCOME FROM COMMISSIONS AND FEES

Many, many properties — and these include huge shopping centers, multi-story apartment buildings, and major industrial parks — are owned by partnerships. You probably won't start out using partnerships as I did, but I thought I'd mention it here to remind you of their potential.

Later, we'll discuss the procedure for setting up partnerships. While state laws differ, you usually can claim a fee for putting partners together. (You can't take a fee, however, for acquiring or selling property for other people unless you're a licensed broker or salesperson.) Check your state laws before writing into the original agreement a fee for bringing the deal to the table.

Here's another fee: Partners know that whomever manages the property, whether it's you or an outside company, is entitled to a management fee. So it might as well be you. Again, check with your state licensing authority to determine if a license is necessary.

And another one: Think about obtaining a real estate license. What it can do for you is expose you to many more available pieces of real estate, before they're publicly advertised, and if you have that license, you can get part of the commission when you buy property listed for sale by a broker. However, a caveat: When you're buying property on your own behalf, you will have to disclose that you are a licensed agent . . . and that can be a negative.

But for the love of heaven don't ever think you should wait until you have a real estate license to start making money in the marketplace. The great majority of individuals who have profited from my home study course and amassed wealth — sometimes *great* wealth — not only have never bothered with a license but have never even considered getting one. You don't need it to make my system work.

Think of a real estate license as an assistant, not as a prime mover. In brief: You don't need it; but if you get it, you can do what one of my "students" told me he does, now that he has a real estate license: He manages other people's properties (you don't need a license to manage your own properties but you do if you're managing for other people), and he's netting an extra $4,000 every month in management fees.

DON'T LET THESE TERMS THROW YOU:

"Instant equity" . . . "Mortgage amortization" . . . "Equity Build-Up"

What does the phrase "instant equity" mean?

We know what "instant" means. (Immediate.) We know what "equity" means. (The value of something minus what you owe.) Putting the two words together, if you're able to buy property below its actual market value, Bingo! You have instant equity.

How do you do that? I'll explain.

One obvious way is by paying all cash. You can make an offer a lot of sellers can't refuse. But wait a minute . . . if we've been talking about no money down, where does the cash come from? From partners, if you choose to go that route and can show your partners that this is a good investment. (An astonishing number of people have extra cash they'd like to invest, if the investment seems logical and potentially profitable.) Use your brains and their money; everyone wins.

You can get instant equity when you make a favorable buy. A couple gets divorced and sells their home to you below its actual market value, *because you're right there with a firm offer.* An executive gets transferred; you buy the house below its actual value, *because you're right there with a firm offer.* Someone runs into financial troubles and sells a property to you below its actual value, *because you're right there with a firm offer.*

In cases like these, when you buy a piece of property below its actual value, you pick up instant equity. You also can get a quick equity by making just a few easy but strategic fix-ups that dramatically raise a property's value. In a later chapter of this book I'll share some really profitable quick and easy fix-up ideas I've discovered over the years.

Now, how about mortgage amortization?

Tricky term, isn't it? Not really.

Here's information you probably already know: When you take out a mortgage — say, the typical 30-year mortgage, which means the mortgage is amortized over 30 years — the first year, more than 99 percent of the money you pay back to the bank or mortgage company is *interest*. That first year . . . and for that matter, the first five years . . . the amount of *principal* you pay off is nominal. You're paying for the use of all that money. Then, as the mortgage-years progress, a higher and higher percentage of your payback goes toward principal payments . . . that is, equity buildup.

Mortgage amortization or equity build-up can be a significant contributor to your net worth, especially if you have a large number of properties and set up 15-year mortgages.

Another term: "Profit and income from selling right."

We're investors. Keep that in mind with every transaction. When we sell property on a properly structured installment sale, we pay taxes on the money we get *only* as we receive that money. We don't have to pay taxes on the profit we make on the "front end." (Confirm your situation with your tax consultant.)

That makes it possible for us to take our profit over an extended period of time without the heavy front-end burden of income tax.

Don't be intimidated by terms such as *instant equity* and *mortgage amortization* and *selling right*. Understanding them and how they work together will mean more profits for you . . . a healthier cash flow for you . . . greater tax benefits for you . . . and a great future for you as a real estate investor.

THE FUTURE OF CREATING WEALTH OUT OF THIN AIR

I've already pointed out that the value of real estate has gone up on an almost uninterrupted basis ever since anybody began keeping records. In many years the value of real estate went up at a higher rate than the Consumer Price Index.

That's the past. How about the future?

No one knows what the future holds, for *anything* . . . whether we're discussing baseball scores, romance, the cost of peanut butter, the ultimate speed of computer chips, or real estate. But real estate has an edge:

What conclusion can anyone possibly draw, except that since we never will have more real estate than we have today (unless explorers start subdividing the planet Mars) . . . since the string of increases has been constant . . . since the demand for property can only go up as population increases . . . real estate will continue to be a solid and steady generator of wealth!

Some nay-sayers, some prophets of doom, say the golden days are behind us. In the 1970s, with double-digit inflation, increase in property values was almost automatic. But it's tough to make money in real estate today.

Oh, yeah?

In this book the editors are quoting just a tiny fragment of the communications from people who have added to their net worth and monthly cash flow, just from applying the principles I recommend. *Not one* of them was in the business in the 1970s when inflation was at a double-digit level.

The profits are there now!

Here's an instant quiz: Over the past hundred years, when interest rates were high, what happened to rental demand?

Answer: Rental demand went *up*. Why? Because families weren't able to buy homes. So generally, an increase in interest rates was accompanied by an increase in demand for rental housing.

So, conversely, if interest rates went down, the demand for rental units went down, because demand for

Both my wife and I work for the U.S. Postal Service. We bought your course to help provide for our retirement, knowing we'd want to do a lot of traveling. Within 3 months, our net worth has gone up $135,000, and we earn an extra $800 a month positive cash flow. We even got over $25,000 cash at closing, on one deal. Not bad, for just a high school graduate! One of my greatest accomplishments in life, which I was able to do through your course, was help my daughter and her husband get into a home of their own. A prouder father there never was!

— *Mike Sano, South Carolina*

houses went up. But the 21st century may be a different game. We have an anomaly: In the late 1990s, interest rates, when they dropped to low levels, did *not* create a significant increase in housing demand.

Why the change? Because most recently, a lower interest rate didn't mean more people could afford to buy houses. What caused it? Credit cards? The demand for more expensive automobiles? Consumer debt seems to reach a new high each year. More and more people have discovered they can't afford to buy the home they thought they could afford.

But a more subtle factor has been at work: Big companies with thousands of employees announce a reduction in their work force of 20 to 30 percent. "Job security" can't be taken for granted any longer. That, too, softens the real estate market. People are afraid.

What a break for us as real estate investors! As every facet of business, finance, and personal security becomes sensitized to interest-rate changes in this country . . . as fear of those changes permeates the marketplace . . . our position as real estate investors gets better and better.

Think of it! Interest rates are down and yet the demand for rental housing is up. If that doesn't suggest *opportunity* I don't know what does. The consumer who normally might buy one of the available properties to live in isn't our competitor in making an offer.

So let's answer the question:

Can you really create wealth out of thin air?

Absolutely.

When you combine equity buildup with appreciation in property value . . . instant equity, where you're buying below market value . . . positive cash flow . . . and tax advantages . . . these add up to *wealth*. And all of these benefits are coming from property purchased with little or none of your own money.

You'll acquire one property, then another, then another, then another. It doesn't happen all at once, but it does happen. Somebody pointed out that you eat a cow one hamburger at a time. You build wealth by picking up one property at a time. (Actually, you can accelerate the pace as you go along, which you can't do when eating hamburgers.)

But I have to repeat, again and again:

This is *not* a get-rich-quick, push-a-button program. You're thinking right if you consider it a get-rich-slow program. But rich is for sure and "slow" is a word you control. Depending on how dynamically you charge into the marketplace, "slow" can be six months or six years.

THE APPRECIATION ACCUMULATION TABLE

I've reprinted here the Appreciation Accumulation Table that comes with my home study course.

Take a look at it. Take a *hard* look at it. Don't move on until you understand what it represents, because it represents a goal you can achieve.

Get-rich-slow? Well, maybe . . . if you consider having a net worth of more than $1 million within ten years slow. (But, how long will it take you to accumulate a million dollar net worth if you don't start investing in real estate? A lifetime? Could you even do it?)

Suppose your goal is to have that million dollar net worth in ten years. Look at the last column, the one under Year "10." Find the figure closest to $1 million: That's $962,000.

Now go to the left column opposite $962,000. The number there is $300,000. All you have to do to reach that $962,000 is buy property worth $300,000 a year. That's just

APPRECIATION ACCUMULATION TABLE

Assumptions
1. Properties acquired at the then-current, fair market value
2. Appreciation 5% annually
3. No principal amortization

Year	1	2	3	4	5
Value of Property Acquired Annually					
$50,000.00	$ 2,500	$ 7,600	$ 15,500	$ 26,300	$ 40,100
100,000.00	5,000	15,300	31,100	52,700	80,300
150,000.00	7,500	22,900	46,500	78,800	120,200
200,000.00	10,000	30,500	62,000	105,100	160,400
250,000.00	12,500	38,100	77,500	131,400	200,500
300,000.00	15,000	45,800	93,100	157,700	240,600
350,000.00	17,500	53,400	108,600	184,000	280,700
400,000.00	20,000	61,000	124,100	210,300	320,800
450,000.00	22,500	68,600	139,500	236,500	360,800
500,000.00	25,000	76,300	155,100	262,900	401,000

Year	6	7	8	9	10
Value of Property Acquired Annually					
$50,000.00	$ 57,100	$ 77,500	$ 101,400	$ 129,000	$ 160,400
100,000.00	114,300	155,000	202,700	257,800	320,700
150,000.00	171,200	232,300	303,900	386,600	480,900
200,000.00	228,400	309,800	405,300	515,600	641,400
250,000.00	285,500	387,300	506,700	644,500	801,700
300,000.00	342,600	464,700	607,900	773,300	962,000
350,000.00	399,700	542,200	709,300	902,300	1,122,400
400,000.00	456,800	619,600	810,600	1,031,100	1,282,700
450,000.00	513,800	697,000	912,000	1,160,100	1,443,100
500,000.00	571,000	774,600	1,013,300	1,289,000	1,603,400

four average properties over the whole year. Some people buy two dozen or more. Still, others just buy one larger multi-unit building every year or so.

If you keep going for 20 years, you'll have between $2.5 million and $3 million just in appreciation . . . and that doesn't take into consideration your cash flow, your mortgage pay-down, and your tax shelter savings. How's that for a retirement nest-egg? And remember, this is based on buying properties with none of your own money.

Note the three "Assumptions" at the top of the page. They're quite conservative. We aren't talking about buying properties at *below* market value but at fair market value. We aren't talking about huge appreciation. It's just 5 percent. And we aren't talking about picking up instant equities. If you do buy some of the properties at below market value . . . or if appreciation exceeds five percent . . . or if some of these offer instant equity . . . then it's entirely possible you'll be closer to $2 million than $1 million, or, you'll cut your timetable in half!

So the formula is right there in your hands: You buy $300,000 worth of property a year. If the average bread and butter, single family home in your area is $75,000, that's one rental house every three months. You certainly should be able to meet that goal without difficulty. Without difficulty? Let's be more specific: It's easy.

To buy that one property every three months, you may have to call 50 sellers . . . perhaps look at 25 properties . . . maybe make 10 to 15 offers. Really, the time involved is negligible and after your first few calls your procedure will be semi-automatic . . . if you know what to say and do. Later, I'll share with you one of my most valuable assets — my, time-tested list of questions to ask sellers over the phone, to pre-qualify the seller and the property. These can literally save you years over your investing career — and grow your bank account to unbelievable highs.

But you have another important benefit!

As you're accumulating that substantial net worth, you'll constantly have a spendable income from these properties . . . income well up into five or six figures.

After you've been investing for a year or so, you won't have to look at 25 properties or call 50 sellers to pick up one property. You'll have a feel for the business you can get only from having been in the business. And you might start going after bigger fish. One apartment building might represent $300,000 in a single transaction. You're covered for the year!

And if you can buy eight properties a year — that's just one every 6½ weeks — in 4½ years you'll have a $500,000 net worth. But keep going: Assuming the average house is three or four bedrooms, one or two baths, selling for $75,000, if you pick one up every 6½ weeks, in addition to building great wealth you'll have a positive cash flow — that's *net income* — of potentially $55,000 a year, *in addition to* the money you're accumulating as net worth. A great many folks, who have taken my course and become real estate investors, are enjoying incomes of $100,000 a year or more.

No wonder so many quit their old jobs and are now concentrating on the big money to be made as real estate investors!

CHAPTER FIVE

Yes, You *Are* (Or Quickly Can Be) A Seasoned, Credit-Worthy Investor!

(Suggestion: As you read this crucial chapter, make notes of the points you regard as important. Then, after completing the chapter, give yourself a short "self-test" on those points. You'll find you've locked them into your mind — and increased the confidence level you have regarding your ability to achieve success in real estate — far better than you would by passive reading.)

ACCENTUATE THE POSITIVE.

Help yourself. If you were taking my home study course, you'd have automatic "check-points" along the way. This is a book. *You* have to supply those check-points.

Chapter by chapter, you are absorbing the knowledge and skills that I've proved, over and over again, carry the seeds of wealth . . . sometimes *great* wealth. In fact, in this chapter, you'll read about a fellow who started with nothing — zero — and now has a net worth way up there in the millions, strictly because he understood and followed the same principles I'm about to disclose to you.

85

Okay, I know your next question, if at this point you're less than totally convinced.

Your question is: If it's so easy, so obvious, so simple, so absolute, why isn't everybody doing it? Why isn't the guy next door on the phone, buying property? Why aren't all the good deals already spoken for?

Those questions are easy to answer.

Just about every human being in every civilized country on this planet knows that real estate is the best and safest investment. Governments can print money but they can't add land. Stocks and bonds may be fun to own . . . but people can't live in them. Over a period of time (sometimes a very short time — weeks or a few months) real estate appreciates in value. You can lose every dime in Las Vegas or in the stock market, but you just can't lose it all in real estate. Real estate has value. And as I said, everybody knows it.

But there's something they don't know that you're about to learn.

They think you can't get started in real estate unless you have a big chunk of cash to start with. Assume there's a home priced at $100,000, and that it's a bargain at that price. But with a great deal of luck you'll still need $10,000 as a down payment, and that's with a walloping good credit rating. Without a great deal of luck you'll need $20,000 cash to plunk down. And without a good credit rating — well, it's at least a 30 percent down, or forget it.

That's what *they* think. And it's why they're out there, either slaving away to save enough money for *one* down payment on *one* house or dreaming of what might have been . . . while you'll be out there, making deal after deal and raking in profit after profit. A $10,000 quick turnaround profit? Once you're rolling, you'll regard it as "standard operating procedure." For that matter, quick turnaround profits of $40,000 to $50,000 aren't that unusual. As you'll see, a great many others can verify that, yes, quick big profits are standard operating procedure . . . for those who know what they're doing and go about their business aggressively and with confidence.

That's you, isn't it?

In 90 days, our net worth has gone from zero to $430,000 as a result of your course, and our positive cash flow is about $2,300 a month. I am three years ahead of my goals — three years! The goals I wrote down, I blew them out of the water within 60 days.
— *Mike and Gina Maddox, Kansas*

YOU DON'T HAVE ANY CREDIT OR A DOWN PAYMENT? SO WHAT?

I really do want you to have this credo in your mind as you get started:

You don't need a down payment or good credit to buy real estate.

I wasn't the least bit surprised when a fellow without any credit, who attended one of my seminars, came up to me and reported that he had just bought a piece of property, listed at $360,000, for $320,000 — with *no* money down. He proved to himself what I've been preaching for years: *You don't need credit or cash to buy real estate.*

And just today, as I write this, I learned of another student who just bought an apartment complex for $3,300,000 with $25,000 down. The $25,000 was borrowed from a partner, and with a positive cash flow from the property in excess of $4,000 a month, he will be able to pay the $25,000 back, with interest, in less than 7 months. No, you don't need credit to buy real estate.

Many people don't have a "bad" credit rating; they just don't have any *significant* credit rating.

A nasty trend seems to have been established: People are borrowing money and spending it on *destructive* assets rather than *constructive* assets.

Here's what I mean by that:

A destructive asset is one whose value goes down the minute you buy it — cars and boats and trailers and clothes and appliances and electronics. People are literally driving their net worth down the highway; and every day, the value of that car depreciates a little more.

On the other hand, borrowing money for a constructive asset — one whose value is going up — means that money is working for you.

Please understand, even if your credit is bad, you still don't need a down payment to start investing in real estate. But certainly, you should start establishing (or re-establishing) a healthy credit rating as you go, because the number of opportunities that can come your way will go up dramatically.

Please take this suggestion seriously: Visit your local credit bureau. (Every municipality of any size has at least one credit bureau.)

This is especially important if you've been turned down for credit recently. It's too bad that some people who are turned down for credit just shrug and walk away. They never bother to find out why.

You have a lot of rights you may not be aware of or haven't been taking advantage of. First of all, if you've been turned down for credit you can ask the credit bureau for a copy of your credit report, *free*. That's part of what they're required to do.

It might be that some bill you've contested has resulted in a negative report. It might be some long-forgotten dispute. You can find out, quickly, just what your credit report shows. It may show nothing, if you've never asked for a credit card. (Credit card companies usually check with one of the credit bureaus before deciding whether to issue or withhold a card.)

Even if you haven't been turned down and can't get it free (which means your credit report will cost you a few dollars), get it. Understand: The three major credit bureaus — TransUnion, Equifax, and Experian — don't make judgments. They just *report*.

So what do you do if you find something negative that you can explain, by illness or job change, for example? You do this: Write to all three credit bureaus, explaining what the problem was. That can mitigate any adverse information.

In the Appendix of this book I include a sample of what a credit report looks like and, more valuable, tips on how to interpret it. I also list the home office addresses of all three credit bureaus. You may not need any of this, but if you do it's there for you.

If you're seeking to borrow money, you want to make yourself look as good as possible with some honest "puffery." For example, if you're self-employed, "Company executive" seems to be heavier creditworthy evidence than "Self-employed." And "Administrative Assistant" sounds a lot better than "Secretary."

I'll explain why you should have a credit card. But if you just don't qualify for a major credit card like VISA, MasterCard, American Express, or Discover, try getting a proprietary card from a department store, a card the store issues, one good only for purchases in that store. Such cards are considerably easier to get than a major credit card, yet they perform a valuable function: You can pyramid that card into a group of cards, which lead to "peripheral" cards you can use to establish major credit.

And if you have credit cards, try to increase your credit limit. Often, the credit card company will increase your limit just as a result of your asking for the increase.

---

*A tip that will pay for this book many times over: If you are **paying an annual fee**, simply call your credit card company and ask them to delete the fee. Tell them you have other credit card companies that have offered you a no-charge credit card. Chances are they will cancel your annual payment as a result of your asking.*

CASH CAN BE THERE WHEN YOU NEED IT

Today, a $2,500 credit limit on a card is very low. Some cards start you at $5,000. But suppose you have a VISA and MasterCard, with a $2,500 limit on each one. Because you have those cards, you should have no trouble getting a Discover card. That gives you three cards, each with a $2,500 limit, for a total of $7,500.

Now, say you've used $1,500 and are paying each month on that amount. You have another $6,000 you can get, immediately.

So, let's say you come upon a real estate opportunity (and don't jump in yet, because we're just getting started) that costs $50,000, with 10 percent down. No problem: You could use $5,000 of your $6,000 credit line, and *you potentially can own that property.*

Don't go rushing to the newspaper looking for ads just yet. Here is why: Borrowing against your credit line should be a backstop, **not a primary procedure,** unless you see a piece of property you know you can turn over fast for a substantial profit. In that case, the interest you'd pay would be nickels and dimes compared with the big chunk of cash you'll get when you re-sell the property.

A major tip: Generally, you're better off using your credit cards to fix up the property, not to buy it.

THE CREDIT PURSUITS TECHNIQUE

Talk about a paradox! You go to a typical bank to borrow money. You fill out form after form and supply document after document. Then the bank tells you, "Gee, we're sorry, but we can't loan you the money because you don't have enough money for us to loan you money."

What a "Catch-22"! If you had the money, you wouldn't have gone into the bank asking for money in the first place.

Believe it or not, a technique does exist that will give you a line of credit at your bank, or another bank. Let's follow it. I call it the Credit Pursuits Technique:

First, call not just one bank, but several. You have one question any bank officer can answer in ten seconds: "Tell me what your minimum installment loan is." (It might be $500 or $2,500, or whatever.)

Next: Go to that bank and get a Certificate of Deposit equal to that amount. Suppose the minimum installment loan is $1,000. You purchase a $1,000 Certificate of Deposit.

Where do you get the $1,000 to buy the Certificate of Deposit? Chances are if you don't have $1,000 you can borrow it, because the Certificate of Deposit is instantly convertible to cash. Whoever loans you the money is taking practically no risk at all, because the loan money becomes cash on deposit at a bank. Or you might use $1,000 of your credit card line of credit.

If you can round up $3,000, go to three banks and buy a $1,000 Certificate of Deposit at each one.

The benefit of having these CDs is the difference between walking into a bank nervously with your hat in your hand and walking in as a depositor.

Now, here's why you want these CDs:

You walk in as a depositor. You say to the bank officer, "I'd like to talk with you about an installment loan from your bank, of a thousand dollars . . . and by the way, I think I'll pledge my thousand dollar CD in your bank as collateral for repaying that loan."

Can you imagine any bank officer, anywhere on this planet, turning down a deal like that? It has to be the safest loan the bank ever issued, because it's guaranteed by money on deposit right there in their own bank. So you get the thousand dollars. Then you do the same thing at the other two banks. You walk out with $3,000 in cashier's checks, or for that matter, cash.

> When we began, we had nothing and were living from paycheck to paycheck. In the first nine months, we bought 12 properties. All this in a year in which we also had a baby! Our positive cash flow is over $4,000 per month *after* everything is paid!
>
> Carleton, your offer form is great. We own eight properties now, and we've already "flipped" seven and made between $10,000 and $30,000 cash on each.
>
> We've both decided to become real estate brokers, but we still use your offer form in our investing because *it works!* And the investing knowledge we have is from your course, not from our broker education. Besides, we only get 10 percent of our income from being agents. Ninety percent is from using your system. And in everything we've done, we haven't used any of our own money — because we didn't *have* any to start!
>
> — *Tim and Tina Clark, Tennessee*

So let's review. It's as simple as A-B-C:

A. You borrow money from a family member or close friend, or against your credit card line of credit. Use the borrowed money to purchase the CDs.
B. You then take out installment loans for the same amount, using the CDs as collateral.
C. You have $3,000 in cash.

Now, we aren't stopping there. The idea isn't to merely walk away with $3,000.

The bank will give you or send you a coupon book or a statement, indicating your monthly payment. The trick: Don't wait a month. *Immediately* make the first monthly payment. Then, a week later, make the second monthly payment. Then, another week later, make the third monthly payment.

Three weeks have elapsed. You've made three monthly payments. From then on, you make monthly payments as they're called for. Why have you prepaid three months, and where are you getting the money to do all this?

Almost all of it comes from the money you've borrowed to begin with. When you make your payments, those payments become a permanent part of the credit rating you're building. Yes, you're paying a few dollars each month in interest, but your CDs are earning almost as much in interest as you are paying. The benefit to you so far outweighs the handful of dollars difference that no comparison even makes sense.

Once you've paid off the loans, you cash in your CDs and pay back whomever loaned you the "seed" money. You're even. And here's where the whole procedure begins to pay off: You now go back to the bank or banks. This time you're strolling in as a good customer with an excellent credit history. This time you tell the bank officer you want another loan, unsecured.

THE VALUE OF ESTABLISHING CREDIT

Yes, you can succeed without establishing yourself as positively credit-worthy.

No, it isn't as easy, as quick, or as profitable as if you *had* taken a few steps to build a little credit and a little bit of a reputation. But look what you've done: From a point of absolute zero, and without having any front-money, you've not only built a credit history; you've become credit-worthy!

Once you're a real estate investor, simply by identifying yourself as a real estate investor, you can get a surprising amount of attention from suppliers and tradespeople . . . and a surprising number of discounts as well. Just ask! The simple two-part rule:

Credit breeds credit. "Position" breeds discounts.

I certainly don't have to tell you that you won't get credit or discounts unless you ask for them. This parallels the rates hotels charge for rooms. The typical individual walks in and pays what they call the "rack rate." That's the listed rate, and the listed rate obviously is the highest rate they can charge. The individual with position walks in and asks for the corporate rate. Immediately, that rate saves him or her 20 percent or more, for the same room. The person who has strong established credit walks in with a "Platinum" card and may get a free upgrade or late checkout or a free breakfast or other "perks" the typical person without that signal of top credit and top position cannot qualify for.

I'll re-emphasize: You *don't* have to build up a credit history to buy real estate. In fact, if you declared bankruptcy, even earlier today, you still can buy real estate with no money down. The purpose of having good credit is to expand your opportunities and enable you to achieve your financial goals faster.

Three years ago we had filed for bankruptcy. We had no credit whatsoever. We asked some people in our church to help us get a mobile home financed. That's all we could afford. With the help of your course, we got our credit established again. This is a check for $1636 that we got at the time of closing on our four-unit rental property. Absolutely no money down, nothing. Even our kids can't believe Mom and Dad are doing these things. We went from absolutely nothing to where we have almost every major credit card in the world — VISA, Discover — we have them all.

— *David and Renee McElveen, Michigan*

ESTABLISHING YOURSELF AS A SEASONED INVESTOR

Those who have completed my home study course tell me over and over again: "I couldn't believe I could do it, but I've established myself as a seasoned investor." I realize this is a book and not the full home study course, and I realize that the full course has thousands of explanatory elements no single volume could possibly include; but what *you* should realize is that others, many of whom started out not only with nothing but, in some cases, with *less* than nothing, are cashing big checks every month of the year. And they didn't have to labor for five or ten years to bring this about.

One key is to learn the words investors use — the "lingo." You don't want to sound like an outsider when you're acting like an insider.

Another is to establish a businesslike ambience. You don't need to rent an office, *but* you do need to be organized, whether you're using a desk or the kitchen table. Nothing is more discouraging (and less professional) than having notes and documents scattered all over the place. Think in a professional manner: If you rented an office and hired a secretary, wouldn't the papers be orderly? Wouldn't you have a time schedule? Wouldn't you know where things are? You *don't* need an office nor a secretary to be organized.

When I first began explaining my techniques and strategies, fax machines were an expensive luxury. No longer. Businesspeople conduct business by fax. If you have to hand-deliver messages, you're an amateur; if you have to mail them, you'll often be too late to be effective. But businesspeople demand, "Put it in writing." So get a fax machine. Today a good one costs no more than a few hundred dollars . . . some even less . . . and as a real estate investor, you may be able to shave that price or buy wholesale. At worst, pick up a used one for almost no money. Today's business, on all levels, demands a fax machine.

And you don't need a dedicated fax line. An inexpensive gadget "senses" whether the call is a phone call or a fax and refers the signal to the proper instrument; so you can use the same telephone line you now have.

If you do have a few extra dollars, investing in a second telephone line — which becomes your *business line,* one you may want listed that way — can be a big asset, because it represents proof to outsiders that you are what you claim to be — a genuine, real, authentic, bona fide real estate investor. So much business is conducted lightning-fast, by phone or fax, that you'll miss out on many, many opportunities unless your you are professionally competitive.

All right: Let's talk turkey!

TECHNIQUES TO GENERATE CALLS FROM SELLERS

Before we discuss this very important section, a disclaimer: Nobody bats a thousand, not even the best batter who ever played in the major leagues. You're buying property without putting up cash. Others are buying property *and* putting up cash. Does that leave you at a disadvantage? Sometimes. But before you've finished this book, you'll see how easy it is, at other times, to convince *some* sellers to deal with you. And you make money. So don't worry if a particular seller isn't interested, because, believe me, plenty of others *will* be interested. In fact, instead of your calling them, *they'll* call *you.*

How do you get somebody who's ready to sell a piece of property to call you, so you can make an offer? In my home study course I explain nine different techniques. Even without the course, if you have some background or instinct in salesmanship, you may know (or guess) at least one or two of these. For example . . .

An absolute *must:* business cards. Contact a local printer or office supply store and get some cards printed up. You don't need multi-colored, embossed, or engraved cards. For a handful of dollars you can get 500 or a thousand cards.

Carleton, in 1989 we declared bankruptcy. We were renting. We were bankrupt, we'd lost the house, and we were having a child.

I was determined that I didn't like where I was at, and I was worried that now that I had a second child on the way, I needed to do something and I needed to do it in a hurry. So, we got your course.

Your course — it taught me how to organize myself. That's the biggest thing. Because you can overcome a lot of barriers if you get everything organized and get a plan.

We developed in just a short few years, $385,000 net worth and a spendable cash flow of $44,000 a year.

You unknowingly have unleashed some abilities that we didn't know we had. Anybody could do this. It's just a matter of organizing, setting a plan, and improvising, just a little bit and go for it.

— *Carl and Rose Delabar, Georgia*

What do you put on the cards? Your name, obviously, plus address, phone, and fax number. You might also include a company name if you have one (but *don't* make one up. It should be registered, because Murphy's Law says the name you make up will belong to another person somewhere, and that means trouble), although a company name can actually turn off some sellers. Better than a company name is a statement of what you do: "I buy properties" or "I buy houses." That's straightforward and inspires trust, where "International Real Estate Consortium" can cause a seller to think you're some sort of conglomerate that will take advantage of him.

So what do you do with your business cards? Give them to just about every adult you know, every business you deal with. Every delivery person, mailman . . . everyone. Get the word out!

Can you work with real estate brokers? Sure, you can.

A broker has to have a license, and you don't. But that license doesn't make the broker any wiser or better-educated or even more knowledgeable about the real estate business than you are.

You can and should establish rapport with as many real estate brokers as you can. Your best contacts are brokers who have themselves owned investment property. You represent fast, aggressive action, and any broker likes that attitude.

So start cultivating brokers. You'll find, as you've found throughout your life, that you'll hit it off well with some and just not have any "chemistry" with others. You know what to do: Work to intensify the relationships with those with whom you have rapport. Don't waste your time with those who seem cold and distant and disrespectful of what you do. That isn't good business practice for you. (For that matter, it isn't good business practice for them either, but that's their problem, not yours.)

Another tip: Go to garage sales. Almost half the people who hold garage sales are thinking about moving. Pass out your cards: You're there first! In fact, you might generate an opening discussion on the spot.

Cards are cheap advertising. Cards are professional advertising. Use them, and don't be afraid to tell the people, "If you know anyone who's interested in selling his or her home, tell that person to call me."

Run a few ads in the most inexpensive media in your area. Neighborhood newspapers usually are good buys. And don't get tricky with the wording. The person looking for a straightforward deal will turn away from slick advertising. State clearly and forthrightly why the ad is in the paper: "I buy houses" . . . or "If you're a motivated seller who wants action on your house, call me. I'm ready to deal, and I can offer full market price if you'll be flexible on the terms."

Don't run one ad and stop. Run a "schedule" of ads. You never know when that motivated seller will see your ad. (A peripheral benefit: The more often you run your ad, the less each ad costs.) You don't need a giant ad. A couple of inches, with a heavy border, should do it.

Important: When a seller calls you on the phone and asks, "What do you mean by 'flexible terms'?" **don't** *ever respond directly to that question. Instead, say, "Well, that depends entirely on the situation. Tell me: . . ." and then* **you** *start asking questions. I'll give the time-tested questions to ask later in this text.*

You can use your ad to attract renters or buyers to properties you own. As an aside, if you can develop a friendly and warm telephone rapport with the caller, it is nothing short of amazing the information you are able to learn.

What you can do by being both a buyer and a seller is pick up a group of interested sellers and interested buyers. Where *you* come in is buying the property for no money down and then turning it around for *some* money down.

In my opinion — and my opinion is backed up by over a quarter of a century of doing just this — every seller who has placed a classified ad in the real estate section of the local paper, even in the "For rent" section, is a candidate for you to buy their property with no money down. How? Keep reading.

Some 80 to 85 percent of sellers are "firm" in their price; they are inflexible. In two words: So what! That means 15 to 20 percent are flexible on either their terms or their asking price, or both. These are the ones we want, because these are the ones that enable us to buy property creatively.

Occasionally you'll see an ad that says, in one way or another, "Must sell." Or those wonderful (for us) words, "For sale or lease option" or "Rent with option to buy." Those words tell us we should be able to buy that property for no money down. Another word: "Asking," followed by a dollar amount. That word "Asking" means flexible.

Passing out inexpensively-printed "I buy property" flyers in neighborhoods of homes can bring leads. Passing out inexpensively-printed "I have homes for sale" flyers in apartment buildings can bring leads.

I'll mention banks here, because banks are your source of "REO" properties — "real estate owned." These are foreclosures, and you can bet the bank will be anxious to sell the property. A bank usually won't be interested in absolutely no money down, although some I am familiar with have worked with buyers on those terms; but even $500 or $1,000 down or a lease/purchase arrangement should interest the bank.

Leads are everywhere. Take advantage of them. Let the world know that you're a real estate investor, and the world will come to you.

I'm a barber, and I've never made more than $10,000 a year my whole life. I worked 12 hours a day, barely making ends meet and trying to raise a family. When I first saw your course advertised on TV, I thought it was very inspiring. Later on, I decided I was tired of sitting on the sidelines watching everybody else get ahead. So I decided to order it.

With the help of your course, I now own 10 properties, and my monthly positive cash flow is $1,850 — that's $22,000 a year. Plus, my wife and I just bought our dream house.

I'm 50 years old, and right now I have no plans for retiring. I'm having too much fun. Every place I go, I always look for real estate. I drive through neighborhoods, looking for real estate. I just love it. And I'm making money.

— Ron Hyre, West Virginia

CHAPTER SIX

Knowledge Is Power!

(Suggestion: If you've read this far, it's time for a reminder: Please, please don't just grab onto the highlights of this text and ignore the refinements. You don't have to be a real estate expert; you don't have to know a large number of technical terms; you don't have to sit with this book at your elbow. But . . . you DO have to study your own market to determine which "niches" will be most profitable, and you DO have to have the right knowledge. In three words: Don't invest blindly.)

PROFIT FROM MY MISTAKES

As you saw in chapter 2 of this book, the one sure way to bridge the gap between *theory* and *application* is that magic word *judgment*.

You have the opportunity to profit from the mistakes I made in my earliest days as a real estate investor, when after a few years I thought I had the Midas touch and every piece of property on which I could lay my hands would turn to gold.

No. The "Buy Anything" theory of real estate investing can result in a major disaster. So I propose two oars in
these waters, to steer you on a safe course:

A. Profit from my early mistakes. Re-read chapter 2
   and vow to temper enthusiasm with judgment.
B. Study the marketplace. You'll find that with each
   passing week, both your judgment and your confidence will expand. You'll spot opportunities faster
   and faster . . . and you'll know how to exploit those
   opportunities. I'll show you how to make a "quick
   study" of the field — "shortcuts" so to speak, based
   on my years of experience.

One of the most attractive aspects of real estate investing is that you can base all your decisions on logic. You
aren't a real estate speculator; you're a real estate investor.

The speculator says, "The roulette wheel has come up
red five times in a row. The next spin has to be black." The
logical investor says, "Each spin of the wheel has no relationship with previous spins of the wheel. The next spin
has an even chance of being red or black."

Which of those two is most likely to walk away from
the table having lost it all? Speculation is a guess. In fact,
among the dictionary's definition of the word are: *"reason-
ing based on inconclusive evidence and engagement in risky business transactions on the chance of quick or considerable profit."*

Do you want to make decisions based on inconclusive
evidence? Do you want to engage in a risky business transaction? Does the word "chance" give you a thrill instead of
a chill?

The entire purpose of this book, and my home study
course, is to eliminate as much speculation, as much risk,
as much chance, and certainly as much inconclusive evidence as is humanly possible. Let the speculators take their
chances. You're an investor.

COME ON, LET'S CREATE SOME VALUE

I'll emphasize again . . . and you'll probably see it several more times before you've finished these pages: You *don't* have to be a real estate expert to enjoy huge success. But please don't draw the wrong conclusion: That statement doesn't mean you can sit reading the Sunday comics, then turn to the real estate classified ad section to see what properties are for sale. Study your craft and you'll be that much more ahead.

For example, a key question is whether or not to fix up a property before offering it for rent or re-sale. As a general rule, the answer is: Absolutely.

Let's say you've bought an inexpensive home. One reason it cost so little was that the paint was peeling, the fence had holes in it, the shrubbery around the house was terribly overgrown, and some of the tiles in the kitchen floor were cracked.

What if you spent part of a weekend touching up the paint? What if you repaired that fence so it wasn't falling down? What if you replaced the broken tiles or re-covered the kitchen floor with fresh vinyl? What if you trimmed the shrubs? What might the result be?

You know the answer before I tell you: Not only can you ask more for the house than you paid for it because it appears to be more livable, more upscale, better-maintained, but there will be many more prospective buyers who will show an interest.

In my state of Florida, I often will install ceiling fans where none existed before. What a terrific selling point those fans are, whether to buyers or to renters! The cost is next to nothing, at a building supply store. I can install them myself, but sometimes I'll just hire a handyman and pay him $20 or $25 per fan to install them and add a wall-switch.

Another way to increase the value of a property is through the financing. Think for a moment before reading on: Which is a better property for us to purchase — a property that is 100 percent financed, with no equity, or a property that is owned free and clear?

In the early days, when I labeled myself an investor but actually was more of a speculator, I'd have chosen the property that's 100 percent financed. Not now. Today I'd pick the property that's free and clear, every time. It allows you to be very creative in structuring the financing.

A simple rule applies:
The more equity the seller has in the property, the easier it is for us to acquire the property.

WITH MORTGAGES, DO NOT ASSUME THEY ARE ASSUMABLE

The most favorable financing is financing that's *assumable.* But if you've tried to find assumable financing, you know the market has changed drastically since the "golden" days of the mid-1970s when a great many mortgages were assumable.

Most F.H.A. mortgages written before December 1, 1989, are freely assumable. Today, you must qualify to assume them. Assumable financing from conventional sources like banks and savings & loans, ceased in the mid '70s, and is almost impossible to find. So when we happen upon an assumable mortgage, we know we have an unusually favorable circumstance. Just one caveat: If it's an F.H.A. mortgage and you want to assume it, you have to occupy the property. You might not want to do that, either because it isn't as desirable a place to live as your existing home or be-cause it would mean an abrupt change of lifestyle — new schools, a longer commute, leaving a neighborhood you en-joy, and on and on.

How about V.A. mortgages? None of them written af-ter the end of 1989 are assumable without qualification. So once again, we have a vanishing breed.

How do you know whether a mortgage is assumable? Often, you have to do some research. I don't know why so many real estate brokers don't give us that information in their listings, but they don't.

It's safest to assume the mortgage *isn't* assumable. Once you've checked your belief that it's not and found it to be fact, your next job is to find out how much equity (total value minus money owed) is in the property. Does the seller have a 10 percent equity? A 50 percent equity? The way in which we approach the seller will differ, based on the amount of equity he or she has.

Be suspicious when so-called experts tell you, "There are ways around the assumability problem. You can Lease Option the property or buy on an Agreement for Deed, and that won't trigger the 'Due on Sale' clause."

Nice theory. Just one thing wrong with it: It's ab-solutely incorrect. A Lease Option *will* trigger the 'Due on Sale' clause because the mortgage will specifically refer to "any transfer of legal or equitable title to real estate." If someone gives you a deed, obviously you're getting legal title to the property. If someone gives you a Lease Option or sells property to you on an Agreement for Deed, you're getting equitable title to that property . . . regardless of whether the Lease Option is for six months or ten years or the Agreement for Deed is for 25 years. Equitable title is be-ing passed even though legal title isn't.

But here's a curious point: If there is an Agreement for Deed or a Lease Option, the lender may never know about the transfer of equitable title. Even though the instrument of transfer may be recorded in the public record, it's unlikely that a typical lender makes a regular practice of sending a junior employee to the courthouse to copy a list of properties that have been transferred under the terms of a Agreement for Deed or a Lease Option.

In the case of a legal transfer of title, though, the lender will usually learn of the transfer. How? Simple: The mortgagee — that is, the lender — is named as the co-beneficiary on the hazard, fire, and flood insurance on the property, and the mortgagee will receive a copy of the new insurance policy or certificate.

Look how simple the typical transaction is: "A" is loaning money to "B." As security for the loan, "B" gives "A" collateral. What's the collateral? The property "B" is buying. Proof, evidence of the collateral, is the mortgage. So each party gets something. "B" gets money; "A" gets the mortgage. The *mortgagee* ("A" in this case) is the lender. The *mortgagor* (in this case, "B") is the borrower. In the case of a Lease Option, the *lessor* is the owner of the house. The *lessee* is the one who occupies the property. The *optionor*, the owner of the property, is the one who gives the option; the *optionee* is the one who receives the option.

A short interruption: Does some of this terminology confuse you? Unless you've been in this business for a couple of years, the answer has to be yes. Don't worry about it. You can always keep referring back to this book until you're familiar with the terms. That's one reason I point out that each passing day, week, month, and year will witness an improvement in your comprehension and your style. But don't wait for perfection.

Let's get mildly technical for a moment. (You might want to put a marker on this page, because it can represent an area of profit many investors don't know about or, if they do, they don't consider.) I've never heard of a lender checking into the transfer of a property under the terms of a Agreement for Deed or a Lease Option. But is there a possibility of that happening? Of course there is. Understand, please: Nothing is illegal about the transaction. You just want to be aware of the possibility that if the lender does find out, the lender can "accelerate" the mortgage and call all the money due and payable.

What if that happens? If you actually do get legal or equitable title to the property that has a mortgage with a *Due on Sale* clause, and you don't say anything about it (and they find out about it in the case of equitable title), you'll probably hear from the mortgagee in four to six months. When and if they do, if you've made the payments on time, chances are good that they'll allow you to assume the mortgage without a great penalty, but it's not a certainty.

What's the worst that can happen? The mortgagee will want the mortgage paid off. That can happen when the mortgagee sells the mortgage to investors who insist on the mortgage being paid off.

A sidelight: If you buy a condominium and take legal title to it (getting a deed), that, too, will trigger a "Due on Sale" clause. But from a practical point of view the lenders won't know because of this difference: There's no insurance naming the lender as a co-beneficiary. The insurance is carried by the condominium association. Your only insurance is on the personal property and interior contents.

On many occasions I've bought a condominium under circumstances in which a Due on Sale clause applied. I've never had the sale trigger that clause.

But that's not because the clause isn't valid. Be careful. Be aware of the possibility that under the worst case scenario the lender *could* invoke the clause.

It's one more proof that *knowledge is power.*

WORKING WITH REAL ESTATE BROKERS

Real estate brokers are like doctors and lawyers — they develop specialties. Your best contacts will be brokers who deal in the kind of properties you're looking for — moderately expensive and inexpensive homes — the "bread and butter" properties.

Others may have opportunities for you in condos, in multi-family units, or in quick opportunities where they know you can move fast and decisively even though you may want to negotiate for a no-money-down sale.

As a general rule, you are best advised, where possible, to work with brokers who are, or have been, investors themselves. They will be much more familiar with the entire investing process and as such, will be able to serve your needs more effectively.

(A parenthetical note: Only brokers who belong to the National Association of Realtors can call themselves "Realtors.")

You especially want to cultivate a relationship with agents and brokers who subscribe to the local multiple listing service (MLS) and will share those listings with you. You'll find, too, that you can establish an easy and profitable connection with brokers who have themselves invested in properties.

How does the relationship work?

A broker will get a listing. He or she then puts that listing into the multiple listing service, which makes it available to all brokers in the area. The only way the listing broker can collect the entire sales commission (usually six to seven percent) is to be both the listing broker and the selling broker.

That doesn't happen often. Usually, one broker lists the property and another sells it. So the commission is split, 3 or 3.5 percent to each, and even then, that 3 or 3.5 percent can be split between the salesperson and the owner of the brokerage firm.

Can you see what this can mean to you as a real estate investor? Of course you can.

You're driving through a neighborhood. There's a house that fits your pattern. In front of the house is a sign: "Johnson Realty." Even though you may have a delightful working relationship with Smith Realty, good business judgment calls for you to contact Johnson. That way, Johnson can visualize collecting the complete commission . . . which can be an incentive to deal with you.

Here's the other edge to this sword: Suppose you ask the broker if he or she will be willing to finance the commission and spread the payment out over a period of time. The broker says no. You then say, "Well, I've been working with another broker who is willing to finance his commission." The broker stands firm: "Go ahead and do it." So you approach your friendly broker who *is* willing to finance his commission. The originating broker gets his 3 percent; but if he had agreed to finance his commission, eventually he'd have collected the entire 6 percent.

Why do you want the broker to finance the commission? Because you're dedicated, as much as is possible, to a no-money-down philosophy of property acquisition. After all, why spend your hard-earned money when you can use "knowledge and strategy" to pay the bill.

WORKING WITH A BUYER'S BROKER

Obviously, a buyer's broker is a real estate broker who represents the buyer. Obviously, too, that broker's primary loyalty will be to the buyer (you) rather than the seller.

That the broker represents you doesn't necessarily mean he or she gets the commission from you. It's very possible for the broker to get the commission from the seller, even in this scenario.

Now, you don't have to enter into a formal buyer's broker agreement with a broker to act as your representative; you can enter into an informal agreement to have that broker keep an eye out for property in which you might be interested. While this is not a true buyer's broker relationship, many real estate investors maintain such a relationship with one or more brokers.

The broker might ask for a retainer or a fee, in exchange for being your "bird-dog." Nothing wrong with that, provided you and the broker also agree that when you buy a property, the broker deducts the advances from the commission so you'll start fresh on the next project.

What if the broker wants an exclusive — "For any property you buy, whether from another broker or from an owner, I have a commission coming"? Don't respond to that siren song. You not only become secondary in every transaction, but you cost yourself both your edge and some money. If you buy direct from the owner, one of the "perks" for both parties is avoiding any commissions.

It's certainly true that not all brokers are grist for our mill. Some, in fact, are anti-investor, or at least anti-creative-investor. So what? There are thousands of others who welcome us, because we represent that wonderful word: ACTION.

In the workbook accompanying my regular home study course there's an entire section that deals with how you can constructively and positively work with brokers. In it, I list five guidelines you can transmit to brokers with whom you might be interested in working. You tell that broker you're after . . .

A. Any property owned by a flexible or highly motivated seller.
B. Any property the seller is willing to finance.

C. Properties with mortgages whose outstanding balance is less than 50 percent of the asking price.
D. Any property with an assumable V.A. or F.H.A. mortgage.
E. Any property being offered at 80 percent or less of its fair market value.

Don't count on a huge number of referrals from brokers. You aren't the only one in the marketplace, and a broker who discovers a home for sale at less than 80 percent of its fair market value may try to snap it up directly. But look how easy it is: If you get just four or five referrals every week, you have an excellent possibility of picking up one property a month. That's twelve a year. And that's just from brokers. You also will have your own strategic methods of direct contacts and calls that could triple or quadruple that amount.

A NEW CATEGORY: THE "TRANSACTION BROKER"

This category didn't exist a generation ago. It shows how specialization has filtered into the fast-moving world of real estate.

A transaction broker doesn't represent the seller and doesn't represent the buyer. This broker represents . . . the broker. He or she is an independent contractor who tries to bring together two parties and then collects a commission from whomever will pay it (generally, the seller).

This type of brokerage originated in California and has spread nationwide. The owner of a house may get a cold call or a mailing: "Might you be interested in selling your house?" The Transaction Broker then sets out to find a buyer. The house isn't "listed" in the conventional sense, but the Transaction Broker has an implied fiduciary (a legally imposed duty of trust and confidence) relationship with both seller and buyer.

You can see that a Transaction Broker can be a powerful connection for you as a real estate investor. You're interested in every property the broker can find, provided it conforms to any one of the five guidelines.

A BONUS, AND HOW TO USE IT

My home study course includes a Purchase (offer) Contact that is the culmination of many years of refinement and thousands of dollars in attorney fees. I'm very proud of it. This contract heavily favors the buyer. (Of course it does. You are the buyer, why would it favor the other party?) Most other standard form contracts currently in use favor the seller.

You may submit this contract to a broker, and the broker will say, "Hey, this contract favors the buyer." That has nothing to do with his obligation to present the offer to the seller. If he refuses to present your offer, you have major recourse. You can go to your state's Real Estate Commission and report the broker. *By law, a broker **must** submit any legitimate offer.*

One qualifier: A local broker who is part of a group that uses a standard contract may not be able to use this one. He has to use a prescribed form endorsed by the state Realtors Association and perhaps even the Bar Association or licensing authority. If that happens to be the case, let the broker use his own contract . . . and use an "Addendum" to add the specifics from your buyer's contract. (Incidentally, I give my home study course users my permission to input this contract in its entirety into their computer, to use in each offer they make. In fact, I encourage it. For their and your convenience, I have developed my "Computer Toolkit" Program which has this contract in it, along with a myriad of other forms and "what if" analysis scenarios. It's available in Windows and DOS, for a nominal fee by contacting the Professional Education Institute.)

Your relationship with the broker can pay off when the broker submits the offer. Seldom does the broker just say, "Here," and hand over the offer. As often as not, the seller will ask the broker's opinion. What if that opinion is negative — such as, "Maybe you ought to wait for a better offer"? Or worse: "By law, I have to submit this offer, but it's nonsense"?

We've covered this in chapter 3. Re-read that chapter if you think such a circumstance may occur. As a reminder: Write into the contract, "Buyer reserves the right to accompany broker to present offer." I'm repeating this because a negative broker can kill a deal. That negativity, however, may disappear if you're standing there.

And don't forget to have your address, phone, and fax number on the offer. Sometimes what appears to be a dead deal springs to life *months* later. The seller hasn't moved the property. Your offer is in the desk drawer. You'll get an unexpected but very welcome phone call: "Are you still interested?"

That can't happen if the seller has no way of contacting you.

SHOULD YOU BECOME A LICENSED BROKER?

We've discussed this possibility before.

If being a broker gets in the way of being an investor, don't waste your time and your money.

Understand, though: You can profit from a number of benefits if you do pursue and get a broker's license. One benefit is very general: You'll simply know more about real estate in general. Francis Bacon said, 400 years ago,

"Knowledge is power." And Ben Franklin said, "The best dividends you'll ever receive is on your own investment in education." They were right then, and they are right now.

Specifically, if you have a license you can quickly affiliate yourself with a broker. That immediately gives you access to the multiple listing service. It also entitles *you* to a commission when you buy or sell listed property or when you help other people buy or sell property. (WARNING: One of the *counter*-benefits of working for a broker is that you will *not* be able to point out to the seller: "You'll save the broker's commission, and that's thousands of dollars.")

Too, brokers or agents respect brokers or agents. You'll be able to negotiate on even terms, agent to agent.

Now, on the other hand . . .

Becoming a broker demands an investment in time. That time might well be spent making money as an investor.

And you automatically add a harness to yourself. By law, when you're a broker or a salesperson you have to identify yourself as such. (If you don't identify yourself, and you make money when you re-sell, the original owner might sue you.) The "casual" and friendly one-to-one, buyer-to-seller, disappears. The seller quite rightly regards you as a professional whose investment goals might be more self-serving and more likely to conceal a hidden agenda than would be true of a nice person who just wants to help the seller solve his problem by taking the property off his hands at the best possible terms.

Congratulations! You're well on your way.

In fact, you might now start looking for "bread and butter" properties . . . that is, three or four bedroom properties that are well-located and are priced to appeal to the largest number of people looking for housing. Even though we haven't yet covered the procedure for opening the door to a purchase, who knows? You might strike a gusher, which means you'll have to rush through the rest of this book faster than you planned to!

CHAPTER SEVEN

The Magic of "No Money Down" Over the Phone

(Suggestion: The telephone is not only your friend; if you're a real estate investor, the phone is your partner. Practice your telephone techniques. If you have a tape recorder, tape yourself making a sample call. How many times do you pause with "Uhhh"? How many times do you stumble, having to follow up a mis-statement with "What I mean is . . ." or ask a totally meaningless question? The telephone can make you a lot of money . . . if you know how to use it. And what do you do to learn how to use it? PRACTICE!)

YOU THINK THIS IS OBVIOUS? GREAT!

If you use all the ways to generate leads we've discussed earlier in this text, you positively will be getting some telephone calls.

How you handle those calls has a profound effect on the success of your real estate investing. Look at it from your own viewpoint. When you've called an individual or a business, what impression do you get from the voice on the other end? Confidence? Lack of confidence? Bravado?

119

Uncertainty? Unfriendliness? Cordiality? The feeling the person you called knows his or her business? The feeling that the person you called is a total amateur?

Don't you adjust not only your words but your entire attitude, based on that reaction?

You'll use the phone to determine far more quickly than you could under any other circumstances, whether you have a good or bad seller and a good or bad property. It can be a huge time and money saver . . . if you use it right.

Here's what I've found, a discovery that has made a lot of money (and friends) for me and can make a lot of money (and friends) for you: The value of that remarkable word *rapport* can't be overstated. Thousands, perhaps millions of deals are killed because a negotiator decides to act like a negotiator. What comes out of the other earpiece is an impression of arrogance, disdain, or, worse, an assumed position of superiority.

If you can establish rapport with sellers, the chance of purchasing their property goes way, way up. One technique is, early on, suggesting the seller call you by your first name. You do the same. That seems to establish a relationship. You're buddies, not adversaries.

Avoid asking hostile questions. Be warm and friendly and professional. Remember, you're on a fact-finding mission; you're not, at this point, trying to buy the property with no money down.

One of the most valuable lessons I've learned is one I absolutely propose to you: If a call is unsuccessful, go on to the next one. We learn and learn and learn. We know going in that we aren't going to look at every property. If a seller is unfriendly . . . if a seller becomes irate . . . if the property isn't right . . . so what? The next one is right there, in the dial of your phone. Start fresh with each call and never let your attitude, as you dial the phone, be negative because of what may have occurred in the previous call.

I studied the Carleton Sheets course and started making calls two to three times a week. In late November, I ran across an absolute steal. In December, I closed on a duplex nine years old. The duplex was under contract through Section 8 of the Government Housing Authority.

The mortgage payment was $580.27. I received a total of $853.00 a month from Section 8 which gave me a $272.73 positive cash flow, before other expenses.

In January I renewed my contract with Section 8. Now I receive $1,065.00 a month which gives me $484.73 positive cash flow. Man! I find this hard to believe. I'm still intrigued over the fact that I own property . . . I have been really blessed! Thank you.

— *Kenneth W. Davison, Texas*

THE SELLER INFORMATION FORM

In the Appendix of this book you'll find the Seller Information Form I developed for my own use. Have it next to your phone when you start the day's calls.

(Also, feel free to create your own form. This one works for me, but if you have other ideas, you can't get hurt trying them out.)

The Seller Information Form follows a direct path. I suggest you structure the questions you ask, based on this form. That way you're sure to get enough information to make a valid conclusion.

If the call is useless, you can discard the form. But a more businesslike procedure might be a filing system, especially if you have a computer. One benefit of making a record of the useless calls is that you might build a history of a specific seller. Suppose the person you call is John Jones. You've learned from prior calls that he's inflexible — thus an unproductive call. A month or so later, here's John Jones again. Another unproductive call. When this happens again, you know you have a better use of your own time than calling John Jones. So noting the name and phone number can be a valuable time saver.

Note at the top of the form there are four boxes:

☐ Good   ☐ Flexible
☐ Rejected   ☐ Inflexible

These give you a quick summary. It's possible to amass a fairly sizable stack of forms, and by seeing what you've checked you can have an instant notion of whom you should call back. Also, the forms can be filed numerically by phone number for quick access when you're checking to see if you've called a number before.

The form assures you not only of asking the right questions but asking all the questions you should ask, in order to make your own determination.

The seller may not be able to answer all the questions — for example, neighborhood rent rates. You can determine this information, though, based on prior experience, on other ads in the newspaper, or through a broker.

You'll divide the forms into four groups:

A. Immediate action
B. Call back in 4 weeks
C. Possible future follow-up
D. No action

You know what to do with each group. Obviously, group "A" demands immediate action. You'll take the form with you when you make a personal visit to the property. Groups "B" and "C" should be put into a "tickler" file, marked with a specific date for follow-up, and group "D" just gets filed. (You'll find, though, that now and then you do get call-backs from deals you thought were dead. This is a good reason to have the seller note your name and phone number before concluding the call.)

The biggest single benefit of the form is to save you time. I can tell you from personal experience, I've spent hours, even days, going out to look at properties I never should have wasted my time on. Had I spent a little more time on the phone, *qualifying the property*, that wouldn't have happened. The more information you get over the phone, the less time you're likely to waste on properties that aren't right or where the sellers aren't right.

If you're interested in a helpful video that demonstrates powerful telephone techniques, the Professional Education Institute has one available. The title is: The World's Greatest Telephone Techniques.

I'll tell you my strongest phone success secret: Be an empathetic listener.

This means thinking, "If I were on the other end of this call, what would I be thinking? How would I be answering these questions?" Putting yourself into the shoes — or, rather, the mind — of the person you're calling, trying to understand the problems and stresses he or she may be undergoing, will automatically result in greater rapport. Greater rapport yields greater information and perhaps greater flexibility on the seller's part.

HOW TO MAKE OUTGOING CALLS AND HOW TO HANDLE INCOMING CALLS

In order to get your phone to ring, you need to be aggressive. That means you probably will run ads in the paper. You'll post business cards on bulletin boards. You may even distribute "flyers." You'll get calls from all these.

You can use the Seller Information Form for incoming calls as well as for outgoing calls.

Whether you're calling or receiving a call, have your conversational voice ready. Big-shots don't make it in the world of real estate investing, because the big-shot attitude generates fear: "This guy wants to take advantage of me."

How do you quickly get to a first-name level with the person you're calling? Easy: "Hi. My name is Carleton. May I ask *your* first name?"

Notice, please, it's "Hi," not "Hello." Nothing wrong with "Hello" . . . it's just a little more arm's-length than "Hi."

Your next statement, after learning the sellers' first name: "Please tell me about your home or property." You're after hard information here — number of bedrooms;

My first goal was to buy our home to live in. . . . A Realtor called me back on a 2-bedroom 2-bath condo in a good area. I then proceeded to get the financial data I needed to see if I could even afford the place. Then I started feeling a little awkward in making an offer so I went back to the Carleton Sheets course to build my confidence — and it worked!! I first tried a "no money down" technique. It didn't wash with the seller so I offered to give a $1,750.00 down payment. The seller told the broker to forget it. So, I learned in the course to be firm and let this one go.

A couple of days later I received a call from the broker saying she accepted. "Great things come to those who have patience!" . . . I bought the property below market value and walked into $5,000 worth of equity on my first deal! By the way, my wife and I are only 21 and we're out of an apartment and into our new home!

— *Jeff Gruhler, Nevada*

number of baths; square footage; lot size; whether the house has a garage and if so, for one or two cars; special features such as a fence or big trees; and what furniture and appliances are included with the property.

---

*A major key to successful telephone use: Your first questions should be some they can easily answer, questions **they're** comfortable with.*

The next group of questions can cause problems because the owner may not know the answers: "Tell me about your existing financing?" (You'll want to know what mortgages exist, who the lender is, what the amount of the mortgage is, the interest rate, the amount of monthly payments, and whether the mortgage is assumable.)

Some sellers *will* have the total portfolio at hand — principal, interest, taxes, and insurance. Get as much information as you can. Some sellers may react with, "It's none of your business." Don't get flustered. Simply say, "I'm just interested to know if your present financing could help me buy your home."

If you've built up some rapport, you also can ask whether the seller is current on the mortgage payments. This can be a crucial matter, because a mortgagor (the home owner) who is behind in payments is very likely to be eager to conclude a deal that gets the payments off his neck.

Then you pop a pivotal question: "Are you willing to assist in the financing?"

In most cases you'll get one of two answers: a) "No." b) "What do you mean by that?" Expect a negative response unless the ad you're answering includes wording such as "Seller financing" or "Seller will assist."

You also want to ask whether the seller needs cash at the time of closing and if so how much. What you're after is whether the down payment can be spread out over a period of time. Even though they already have said they won't assist in the financing, they may respond positively to the same question asked in a different way — "Can the down payment be spread over a short period of time?" The word "short" helps prevent a "No." Instead, the typical response is, "How short a period of time?"

Ask yourself which of these is more likely to induce agreement:

- "Oh, say four or five years."
- "Oh, not a long period of time. Say 48 to 60 months."

You can see how the way you couch the answer affects the seller's attitude. You'll find some who will agree. You'll find some who will say, "Well, I can't go that long, but I might work it out over two or three years." What they've agreed to is seller financing for part or all the down payment, whether they know it or not!

THE SEQUENCE OF QUESTIONS CAN AFFECT THE SELLER'S ATTITUDE.

If you're a professional real estate investor your intent should be to convey to the seller, over the phone, that the way you wish to purchase his or her property is good for the seller as well as for you. *Sequence* plays a major role in your ability to do just that.

Assuming the information you've assembled to this point has kept you interested, you'll ask additional questions:

- "How long has the property been on the market?" (Don't expect to get an honest answer to this one every time.)
- "Have you owned the property long?"
- "It sounds like a nice home. I'm curious . . . why are you selling?" (This is a question whose answer, honest or not, gives you an opportunity to be the empathetic listener. If it's a problem or a transfer, empathize: "Wow, that can be tough.")
- "Tell me, what do you like most about your property?"
- "What do you like least about the property?" (You may decide to reserve this question for an actual visit to the property.)
- "Are there any renters in your neighborhood?" (This question serves as a lead-in to your next question, which is a lead-in to the question after it. Progress logically, to maximize rapport and develop information. Avoid implying you're a cold-blooded investor interested only in the numbers, even if you are.)
- "What do you think the rent would be for your property?" (Unless they know for sure, this question usually generates a guessed number that is *lower* than the amount you actually can get when you rent the property.)
- "Would you consider leasing your property with an option to buy?" (Some sellers who absolutely reject the concept of no money down will agree to a lease option . . . which is actually zero interest financing with no money down!) The lease with option technique is one of the most powerful no money down strategies. Much more on this technique later.

Notice how the questions gradually focus in on the target you control. This can't work unless you follow a sequence in which one question leads seamlessly to the next:

"Look, I'm a real estate investor and I'm really interested in your home (or two-family). Let me ask you: If I were able to buy your property for all cash and close on it fast — say, five to seven days — what's the very lowest price you'd consider taking?" ("Taking," not "accepting," because "taking" is active and "accepting" is passive. You're planting a seed: You *could* buy for cash if you chose to, you imply. Almost every seller will quote a lower price than was asked before, but not necessarily the lowest price they will take.)

If a broker is involved, ask the broker: "If I buy this property, would you consider managing it for me? At what rate?" (That's a terrific involvement device.) Also ask: "Do you own any investment property yourself?" "Do you have any properties for sale that might be a good investment for me . . . or maybe some that are physically distressed or whose owner is *very* anxious to sell?" And once you have rapport with the broker, "By the way, do you think you might be willing to take all or part of your commission in the form of a note?"

If the property is being rented, get the broker's opinion of the rental amount. Is it high, low, or about right?

While you're on the phone with the seller and/or the broker, you're filling out the Seller Information Form.

If you decide to visit the property, you will want to add the Property Analysis Form (see Appendix) to the Seller Information Form. You could wind up with more background on the property than the seller has!

My husband, Brent, and I were living in Kodiak, Alaska, where he was a commercial fisherman. He had broken his hand during the salmon season and was unable to work. We had decided it was time for some changes in our lives and that's when we saw the Carleton Sheets program on television. We knew we could do it too! We liquidated our household and began our journey to the "lower 48," closer to family and friends, listening to your program the whole way.

When we arrived, we stayed in a kitchenette motel room and decided we were never going to rent again! We followed your instructions and improved our credit, then soon after, bought our first home — with a mortgage less than rent! When we sold the house, we made a profit of over $13,000.

Our second property, a "bungalow with potential", we bought with no money down from a lawyer. Our efforts in wallpapering, painting, and landscaping paid off. We sold the bungalow and received a check for $46,156!

Our lives have been touched by your program. It really works.

— *Pam MacWilliams, Wisconsin*

A SAMPLER: SOME ACTUAL CALLS

These are transcripts of two actual "cold" calls. My home study course, available from the Professional Education Institute, has the actual voices of these and a number of other calls to individual owners and to brokers.

Telephone Call 1

> Downtown. 3 Bedroom/1 bath. Screened patio. Tenant occupied. Seller will hold mortgage with $5,000 down. Asking $39,000. Realty Company

Man's Voice: Realty Company, may I help you?

Carleton: Yes sir. I was calling about the three-bedroom, one-bath with screened patio that you have advertised in Boynton Beach. Is there anyone there that can help me with that? $5,000 down, $39,000 asking price.

Man's Voice: Yeah, I can get you some information on that. Hang on a second.

Carleton: Okay, great, thank you. (To audience:) While he's getting the information, I'll just comment, we'll still try to learn the associate's name.

Helen: Hello sir.

Carleton: Yes ma'am.

Helen:	I'm sorry about that. My husband asked me to take the call because we've got somebody in the office and he needs to work on the computer.
Carleton:	Oh, I see.
Helen:	Okay.
Carleton:	Would you be able to give me a little information about the three-bedroom, one-bath in the downtown area?
Helen:	Uh huh.
Carleton:	Can you describe the property to me? Are there any special features? I just noticed a three-bedroom, one-bath.
Helen:	It's three bedrooms and one bath, and basically the house is a CBS house (concrete block/stucco), an older home, and apparently there was some fire damage so when they did the repairs on the fire damage, they added an aluminum frame type construction on the side of the house where the other bedroom is. So originally, the house was a two-bedroom, one-bath, and then they added another.
Carleton:	Added another bedroom?
Helen:	Another bedroom with that aluminum construction.
Carleton:	Yeah, does it look like a temporary structure?
Helen:	No, no, it's all secured, and behind that is also a dining room area and a screened patio.
Carleton:	Oh, I see.
Helen:	So that whole section was added and included in the house.

Carleton:	Uh huh.
Helen:	To the house.
Carleton:	Uh huh.
Helen:	And then the kitchen and the living room and the two bedrooms and one bath are in the main part of the house as far as the CBS construction on the original house.
Carleton:	By the way, my name is Carleton. May I ask your first name?
Helen:	My name is Helen.
Carleton:	Helen. Helen, what appliances are included with the property?
Helen:	There's a range and refrigerator being left with the house, along with an air conditioning unit.
Carleton:	Is there a garage or carport?
Helen:	No, no.
Carleton:	Okay. What kind of existing financing?
Helen:	There's no financing on it at this time. He's willing to hold paper on it. He's telling us that when we took the listing that he will hold paper with a $5,000 down payment and a mortgage of approximately 12 percent, but I think he would take less than that for another mortgage.
Carleton:	Yeah, so he's willing to take a $34,000 mortgage?
Helen:	Right.
Carleton:	Yeah. Helen, I'm a real estate investor, and I'm always looking for properties that I think will make good investment properties as rentals.
Helen:	Okay.

Carleton:	Would the seller be willing, you think, to assist even more in the financing than the 34,000?
Helen:	Probably, yeah, he may.
Carleton:	He's a pretty flexible seller then?
Helen:	He sounds like he is. He's living up in Georgia and he's got this property down here. So he wants to get out of management here in the area.
Carleton:	What is the property rented for?
Helen:	Presently it's rented for $450 a month.
Carleton:	Oh, it is.
Helen:	Uh huh.
Carleton:	And how long have the tenants been there?
Helen:	They've been there for quite a while. He tells us over six years.
Carleton:	Oh, for heaven's sakes. Well, that sounds like a pretty good opportunity.
Helen:	Yeah.
Carleton:	How long's the property been on the market?
Helen:	About a month; a month and a half.
Carleton:	Oh, just a month. Has he owned the property long, do you know?
Helen:	From what I understand, yes. As to how long, I don't know, 'cause he said this is the last property that he has here and he wants to liquidate 'cause he wants to get, you know, everything up into the Georgia area, as compared to down here, when he was living here and he moved up that way.
Carleton:	So he's selling because he's an absentee owner?

Helen:	Right.
Carleton:	Yeah. Are there any other renters in that neighborhood, do you know?
Helen:	I don't know offhand. We did meet the lady across the street, and she's been there for a long while. It's an older area, and I'll give you the address on it, and then you can, you know, at least go by it.
Carleton:	Before you do, let me ask you this. Do you think that they would consider lease-optioning the property at all?
Helen:	The present owners or present tenants?
Carleton:	Uh huh. No, the present owner.
Helen:	The present owner?
Carleton:	Yeah. In other words, lease-optioning it to me as an investor and then I would, in turn, sublease it to the tenants.
Helen:	That's possible. That's possible.
Carleton:	Well, it sounds very interesting.
Helen:	Okay.
Carleton:	When I asked you about lease-optioning, do you think the tenant that's in there might want to do that?
Helen:	Yeah.
Carleton:	That would certainly seem to be the way that he might go, I would of thought.
Helen:	Well the tenants originally spoke to them of the possibility of buying it, but I don't think they had enough cash to come up with everything.
Carleton:	Oh, I see. I see.
Helen:	And so, you know, he knew the feasible possibility that the tenants there like the

	house. Of course, if they've been there this long and they like the convenience of it and would possibly entertain working with [the seller.] They might even want to do an equity participation.
Carleton:	Sure.
Helen	Or something like that.
Carleton:	Sure, that sounds very interesting. Helen, let me drive by and take a look at it. And let me also ask you one last question. As you know, if you're a real estate investor yourself, it's important to be able to buy properties and have them make economic sense. One of the ways to do that is to put as little as possible down on them and this sounds very attractive from that standpoint. Do you think that you might be willing to take a portion of your commission in a note?
Helen:	Yeah, that shouldn't be a problem.
Carleton:	Alright, very good. Helen, I'm gonna . . .
Helen:	I also would like you to know that we do specialize in the F.H.A. and the V.A. repossessed properties . . .
Carleton:	Oh, you do.
Helen:	. . . and didn't know if you knew about those types of houses available for sale on a weekly basis.
Carleton:	Helen, let me drive by and take a look at the property and if I decide I want to see it, than I'll get back in touch with you.
Helen:	Okay, and if you're interested in knowing what s available under the H.U.D.

and V.A. repossession list, which also are generally good buys because they're more below market value, give us a call back. Or if you want us to put you on our mailing that we're going to be putting out tomorrow, we'll put you on our mailing list and send out the list to you so that you'd have access to those properties.

Carleton: Alright, let me not burden you with any more mailings than you need and I've got so many too. But, let me look at this property and get back to you. You've been so nice. Thank you; thank you a lot for your time.

Helen: Your quite welcome, Mr. Carleton.

Carleton: Bye, bye.

Call Summary

This out-of-town seller is obviously flexible. The broker is willing to assist in financing by taking a note for the commission. Regrettably, I did not ask if the broker would be willing to go into her pocket to loan money to the buyer to purchase the property. (Believe it or not, some will. You've just got to ask.) With a long-term tenant paying $450 a month, there would seemingly be a positive cash flow on this property despite buying it "no money down."

Telephone Call 2

```
┌─────────────────────────────────┐
│            Windemere             │
│  4BR, 3BA, CBS; built 1983;      │
│  new carpet, tile, fenced        │
│  yard; VA, no qualifying.        │
│  Quick sale at $74,900.          │
│  555-5555                        │
└─────────────────────────────────┘
```

Emily: Hello.

Carleton: Hello. I'm calling about your ad in the newspaper for your four-bedroom, three-bath home.

Emily: Yes

Carleton: Yes, my name is Carleton. May I ask your first name?

Emily: Emily.

Carleton: Emily. Yes, Emily, it sounds like a very nice place. Could you tell me a little bit more about it? Are the bedrooms, for example is it a split arrangement or . . .

Emily: You could say so. When there's three all together, and one in the front.

Carleton: And one in the front?

Emily: But you could use the one in the front, I guess, originally could have been a garage which has been converted, but there's no . . . it looks like the rest of the house.

Carleton: Oh, I see, so there is no garage . . .

Emily: Right.

Carleton: . . . with the property? Any idea what the square footage is?

Emily: Somewhere around 1,700.

Carleton:	Oh, it's a good big house then?
Emily:	Yes. There's more property than anything, actually.
Carleton:	Yeah, when you say more property you mean it's a big yard?
Emily:	A very big backyard, yeah.
Carleton:	Uh huh, and I see it's fenced in.
Emily:	Mm hhh.
Carleton:	Well, can you tell me about the financing? I see it's got a V.A. loan on it.
Emily:	Okay. Around $63,000 assumable. At 11½.
Carleton:	Oh, boy. I remember one time that seemed low. Now it seems high, doesn't it?
Emily:	Yeah.
Carleton:	Yeah. And are all the payments current on it?
Emily:	Yep.
Carleton:	Okay. You're asking $74,900? Would you be willing to assist in the financing, Emily?
Emily:	As far as holding a second, you mean?
Carleton:	Yes, ma'am, or holding a note.
Emily:	Depending on the person, I guess that's where we've got to meet him and talk to him, yeah.
Carleton:	Sure.
Emily:	No doubt about it.
Carleton:	Yeah. Has the house been on the market very long?
Emily:	No, we just now put it in the paper Thursday.
Carleton:	Oh, I see. Emily, how long have you owned the property?
Emily:	A year and a half.
Carleton:	And your monthly payments on that V.A. loan then are pretty high, aren't they?

Emily:	They're $709 [Emily has included the tax escrow in this figure], but that's without Homestead. But, starting this month they're supposed to go down like $30 to $40.
Carleton:	Because of the Homestead Exemption here in Florida?
Emily:	Right.
Carleton:	Yeah. Well, it sounds like you've got a nice place. Why are you selling?
Emily:	Because all of our family lives in Pompano, Coral Springs, and it's a long distance. It's too much to drive.
Carleton:	I see. What do you like most about your home, out of curiosity? It sounds like a nice place.
Emily:	It's closest to where my husband works and the house itself is big enough.
Carleton:	Emily, I'm a real estate investor and I buy properties to rent out. Are there any other renters in your neighborhood, do you know?
Emily:	Um, not that I know of. Not too many people.
Carleton:	Well, if you and your husband talked, do you think you might consider a lease-option? You know, lease the property for a while and then buy it at a later time.
Emily:	Yes and no. We've thought about it, but we kind of rather not. There's this house we're looking at to buy and we'd hold a note for some money, but we would really like to have most of it to put on our own house.
Carleton:	Yeah.
Emily:	That's all the money we would have so . . .
Carleton:	What if you'd hold a note, Emily. How much cash would you need at the time of the closing?

Emily: Well, I guess it's $11,900, so I'll say $5,000 or $6,000.

Carleton: And then a note for the balance. Emily, let me do this. Let me give some thought to it. It's awfully hard to rent out a property, even a nice four-bedroom home for over $700 a month and it sounds like it might not work, but let me give some thought to it and, if I decide I'd like to see it, I'd sure give you a ring back.

Emily: Okay. What are interest rates at now, since you're into all this?

Carleton: What are interest rates? For owner-occupied property, about 8½ percent to 8¾ percent, Emily, and for non-owner occupied, about 9 to 9¼.

Emily: Wow.

Carleton: Emily, I sure do appreciate your time.

Emily: Okay, thank you.

Carleton: Nice talking with you.

Emily: Bye, bye.

Carleton: Bye, bye.

Call Summary

This is obviously a flexible seller. They are willing to accept almost half of their equity in this property in the form of a note.

However, I am familiar with this market area and know that the rental rates here, even though it is a 4-bedroom home, will not support the high interest rate V.A. mortgage loan, plus the other costs of owning this property. We will not follow up on this one.

SUITABLE OR UNSUITABLE?

If you decide the property isn't for you, don't waste any more time. End with a neutral close: "I think I have enough information. If I decide to go ahead I'll get back to you. Thanks a lot for your time."

The seller might even improve the offering price and/or terms then and there. This may or may not affect your decision to look at the property, but it sure would indicate flexibility.

Always leave your name and number. Sellers who don't get the action they think they'll get when they first put the property on the market will regard you as a backstop. Some of them will reach a point at which time is running out . . . and they'll call you.

What if the seller seems inflexible on the terms? Again you thank the seller, leaving your name and phone number in case he changes his mind, and hang up. You might put this in the "tickler" file to call back after six or eight weeks. If the property is still unsold, the seller may no longer be so inflexible.

The Seller Information Form serves a major purpose: It assures you of having all the information you should have. Without it, you easily can overlook any one of a number of significant components that will enable you to make an intelligent and informed decision.

It's a "numbers game." Feeling you have to make a deal on every call puts you at the mercy of the seller and to the negativity of your own frustrated mind.

No!

You might have to make 25 phone calls to end up looking at five properties, making offers on three . . . and buying one. Is that a good percentage?

You bet it is! You easily can make 25 to 50 calls each week, assuming enough ads appear in the paper (including the one you ran). If you buy one property each month, you can wind up with 12 over the very first year. If your goal is to buy just one property, you're already there at the end of the first month!

You don't want to overload yourself; but even more so, you don't want to be so eager to buy a property that you'll break the rules I have laid out and will lay out for you.

If rejection bothers you, then you aren't thinking like an investor. You're thinking like somebody applying for a job.

Are you an introvert or shy? So what! The phone is tailor-made for you, because you're not in a confrontational situation. Many students have told me that they credit the world of real estate investing for springing them completely out of their shells and gaining poise and self-confidence.

You aren't applying for *anything*. You're an investor, looking for property. If you made an offer on an automobile and the dealer turned it down, what would you do? Go to another dealer. That's what you're doing, except the stakes are higher and you're keeping the odds in your favor.

Why not test the waters? Go to the classified section of your newspaper, and make a few calls using my "Seller Information Form". Think about how it feels. Record your calls, as I suggested earlier. Note the progress you'll make

One of my main goals after studying your course was to appear on your TV show to thank you publicly and try to help others believe they can do the same things I have done, and so many others have. (My net worth has improved by $693,950 and I get $103,012 per year positive cash flow.)

This has given my wife and me more freedom, more security, and tremendous respect in our community. I'm happier than ever and have new energy.

— *Dale Francis, Iowa*

from your first call to your third. How did you establish rapport? How did you handle rejection? Did you change the questions to make them more conversational in *your* style? Once you see how you can control your learning, you'll see how then you can control your conversations.

CHAPTER EIGHT

Property Evaluation Techniques

(Suggestion: An ancient rule of psychology: When emotion and intellect come into conflict, emotion almost always wins. "Listen to your gut feelings" is an old admonition. But to be an effective and successful real estate investor, you have to learn to turn off the emotion-switch. "I just love that place" can be a deadly reaction. Analytical materials are at your fingertips. Figure the cash flow. An absolute rule: Your enthusiasm isn't going to turn negative cash flow into positive cash flow. You cannot afford to fall in love with a property.)

WHAT'S IT WORTH?

No professional real estate investor would ever make an intelligent decision — to buy or not to buy — without having a strong analytical indication of what the property is worth.

You're a professional real estate investor. Don't ever try to make a decision to buy or not to buy until you have a dispassionate analysis of what the property is worth. Don't try to guess blindly, especially if you "like" the property.

Emotion will triumph over intellect, and emotion has to stay out of the decision-making process.

In a perfect world, the asking price of a house would be the home's true value. The perfect world, though, doesn't exist. Buyers and sellers alike succumb not only to greed but to the kind of supercharged emotion that can race through an otherwise logical brain. In the case of the seller: "My house is perfect." With the buyer: "I just don't like it."

I'm often amused by the way so many homeowners establish the selling price for their homes. One of the most common procedures is for them to figure what they paid, what inflation has been over the period of time they've owned it, and how much they've spent on improvements. They total these numbers and voila! That's the asking price.

Just one thing wrong with that pseudo-formula: Real estate is only worth what someone is willing to pay for it, not what some formula says it's worth.

A key rule: Money is made in real estate when you buy, not when you sell.

For the buyer, the sole concern should be: How is this property going to benefit me when I buy it? You can see: If emotion creeps into the answer, it isn't an answer at all . . . it's a loaded opinion.

As you look at single-family homes and two- or three-family units, you very well can be competing with other potential buyers who may be looking at the property as a place to live. But, you have an edge over the others: They have an emotional bias. You don't . . . or at least, you *shouldn't*. Their emotional analysis can result in their over-paying for the property. They've outbid you because your

I am pleased to tell you I have just gone to settlement on 10 three-bedroom houses. I managed to find an investor who was ready to retire and I purchased his entire remaining portfolio at a tremendous price. Not only that, but I combined two of the techniques right out of your manual to end up with a total down payment of only $10,000. I paid $5,000 of that at closing with an additional $5,000 due in six months with no interest.

The very best part of this story is that eight out of the 10 houses are already rented and provide me with an instant positive cash flow of over $1,000.00 a month, and that will increase to $2,000.00 a month when I rent the other two.

— *Pete Giglio, Delaware*

evaluation is logical, not emotional, and you aren't about to overpay. Let them have it. Be patient. Move on to the next one. You're in this business to make a profit . . . then let the emotion follow. Believe me, making a profit can give you genuine and well-deserved emotional satisfaction.

WHAT'S MORE UNCOMMON THAN COMMON SENSE?

Lest I emphasize the logical and intellectual side of the decision-making process too much, let me hasten to add that you can benefit greatly from a *common sense* analysis as well. Oh, you can and probably should, at least for your first several properties, hire a property inspector and pay a fee for looking over the property. But as you become more and more familiar with properties and investing, that may prove to be an unnecessary expense. Only you will be able to determine if you need an inspection on a given property.

In my home study course is a "handy helper," a checklist for your common sense analysis. It's a "Buyer's Property Inspection Report," and it covers just about every facet of the inside, outside, and grounds. If your financial analysis is favorable and your common sense analysis is favorable . . . and you're sure you've kept emotion out of the mix . . . chances are the property will be a good investment.

Your systematic and dispassionate inspection of the property not only gains you the seller's respect; but sometimes some of the unsatisfactory entries (again entered without emotion) persuade the seller to adjust down to a more favorable price.

Do *I* use this form in its entirety every time I first look at a piece of property? No, I don't. In fact, sometimes I'll even make an offer sight unseen.

You and I both are busy. If you have a full-time job, going through these steps every time before you make an offer, can be time consuming, and if your offer is rejected, frustrating. So making an offer on property you've never seen can make a lot of sense . . . *under one condition:* You have an out. Allow yourself a contingency (e.g. "Subject to final inspection of the property and written acceptance of same") and the right to inspect the property before the contract becomes final.

AN "INSPECTION CHECKLIST": BUGS, CRACKS, AND MESS

Seven danger signals exist on the outside of a house, and five others can signal problems on the inside.

Number one, for external trouble: Termites.

Termites can cause enormous damage and go undetected for years. Then, long after you purchased the house, sections of wood begin to crumble. You may have to rebuild part of the house, at great expense. A careful inspection for tiny mounds of powdered wood can save you thousands. *This should be done professionally, by others, prior to closing.*

Number two: Dry rot.

Parallel to termites, this problem is unique to wood. Look under eaves. Poke the siding with your finger.

Number three: Cracked foundations. Cracked foundations don't heal themselves. They only get worse.

Number four: Settling foundations. When a foundation settles, two problems result . . . the walls go out of plumb and interior cracks begin to appear.

Number five: Discolored roof sections. Discoloration in itself isn't a major factor. You just want to be sure the discoloration isn't an indication of deeper trouble, such as the need to repair or replace part of the roof.

Number six: Missing mortar from the chimney. This isn't as cataclysmic as some of the others, but it's an indicator that other problems may exist elsewhere because of lack of maintenance. If the chimney seems ready to fall however, it *is* a cataclysmic problem.

Number seven: If the home has a septic system, and the grass is unnaturally flourishing in that area, it suggests the tank may be leaking or not operating properly or the ground has poor absorption.

None of these need kill the deal. Any of these, though, might be a reason to call in a professional, to tell you whether the condition is serious and what it would cost to fix it. That's especially necessary, as I said earlier, if you suspect termite damage.

Understand, as you look for trouble: Some houses are on the market *because* they have problems the owner can't afford to fix. These can be real bargains, and you simply build into your budget the cost of fixing them up.

After you've inspected the exterior, you have five main concerns about the interior.

Number one: Water stains, especially on the ceilings and upper areas of the walls. Water stains are heavy indicators of a leaking roof. While you're inspecting, be sure to include closets. Most closets are located in corners, and corners are where a lot of leaks occur.

Number two: Cracks in wallboards and baseboards. Interior cracks aren't as damaging as exterior cracks, but they can be a red flag to someone to whom you're trying to sell or rent the house. (And, they may be indicative of exterior problems that are not easily seen.)

Number three: Evidence of leaks around window frames. Leaks don't get better. Will you have to replace some frames before you re-sell or rent the house?

Number four: Windows that are difficult to open and close. This problem often occurs in sync with a house that's settled, because the frames no longer are square.

Number five: Leaks and water pressure in the toilets. Actually, it's a good idea to turn on all the water faucets at the same time to be sure the pressure is there and the drains are working. Look particularly under kitchen and bath-room cabinets for leaks.

Chances are, especially in lower-priced houses, you'll find something. Don't expect these houses to be in the same condition they were in the day they were built, just as you wouldn't expect a used car to be in the same condition it was in when the original owner drove it out of the showroom.

The point: These "glitches" can be the reason the house is priced where it is . . . or the reason the owner will accept your offer. Just build into your projections the antic-ipated cost of bringing the house up to standard.

Every decision you make is based on what you've dis-covered and what you anticipate *logically*. Keep emotion out and you'll have a high percentage of proper winners.

In the interest of continuing your education, the Profes-sional Education Institute has recently produced special videos, from my Wealth and Empowerment Training: An In-The-Field Real Estate Investing Experience. *They record actual property inspections.*

These videos really can broaden your range of experience and capabilities. They are real videotaped recordings of a five-day special seminar. With a hotel meeting room as our headquarters, we rented a bus and actually visited almost 20 properties. We in-spected those properties inside and out, commenting on things we noticed, how we'd improve them, what it would cost, and whether each one was economically worth going after. Then we went back to the hotel with our filled-out forms and devised mul-tiple offers to actually make.

What you'll see in the video program is the best of those five days, with healthy doses of instruction, strategy, and tech-niques. I brought in other successful investors, brokers, and mortgage pros to share their wisdom with us. In my opinion, what you'll learn is a very worthwhile addition to the useful time-saving and money-saving information serious real estate in-vestors should have.

THE ROLE OF THE APPRAISAL

I don't usually use an appraiser when I buy property. That's because I think I've reached a point at which I have a pretty good grasp of market value, especially when I'm buying property in an area I'm familiar with.

But when you're just getting started, an appraisal may be a good idea, especially if the property is unique and you aren't sure about its value. Or, if you're using conventional financing, a bank or other lending institution may insist on an appraisal.

An appraiser uses three methods of analysis:

A. Market Sales Analysis. The appraiser checks records to see what similar properties in similar neighborhoods have sold for.

"Similar" includes square footage, age, construction, number of bedrooms and baths, amenities, and size of lot. All this information is available, and you *can* get it yourself if you have the time and inclination to track it down.

(If you have a friendly broker, you'll have access to recent sales — three to six months. Or, as a last resort, all transactions are in the public records, probably in the Tax Assessor's Office.)

Actually, a Market Sales Analysis is a pretty good yardstick. The asking price of other properties doesn't figure into it at all. That number usually represents hope rather than logic.

A Market Sales Analysis is most valuable when trying to determine the value of single family homes. For bigger properties, additional elements have to be considered, as I'll discuss shortly.

If the seller already has an appraisal, look at the date. A professional appraisal is always "as of" a certain date. If the appraisal is many months or several years old, it not only can be outdated; it raises an issue with you: Did the owner get the appraisal in order to establish a selling price, which means the home has been on the market for some time?

B. Reproduction Cost Analysis. This type of analysis tries to compare the cost of building the same type of structure, on land of the same value.

In a Reproduction Cost Analysis, obviously you can't replicate a home that's 20 or 30 years old, so you'd have to subtract for the years of deterioration. Just one caution: Properties age in varying degrees. Some homes that are eight years old have deteriorated far more than well-kept homes that are sixty years old. Some homes have been improved far beyond their original cost, with new siding and plumbing and wiring and roof and built-ins. Subtraction for wear and tear should be thoughtful, not automatic, if you employ this appraisal method. As an aside, fewer and fewer appraisers are using this method.

C. Net Income Approach. This is most valuable when evaluating bigger properties because it's based on an estimate of the amount of income the property will produce.

Net operating income is a term that is vital for you to understand. Net operating income is the amount of income you'd have from the property if you owned it free and clear of any mortgage debt. It is the spendable income if there is no debt. On the flip side, it is your budget for debt.

A rule that can save you a lot of money: If a property can't generate enough income to cover the mortgage payments and expenses and at least break even, do not buy it.

The rule applies to you as a real estate investor. It isn't designed for the typical home buyer, who mixes emotion into the stew of logic. And because the value analysis itself is based on income, this type of appraisal method is most useful when applied to structures of four housing units or more . . . and its usefulness is 100 percent tied to how accurate it is.

A POWERFUL EXAMPLE OF THE DIFFERENCE BETWEEN NET AND GROSS

Real estate investing is a numbers game.

Suppose you come upon a four-family property, available for $100,000, with a net operating income of $10,000. You pay cash for it. You get $10,000 a year — a 10 percent return on your investment.

Now, suppose you're able to buy the same property with a $2,500 down payment. The cash flow, after your mortgage payments, is $100 per month, or $1,200 per year. Which is better?

If you do the mathematics, you can see at once: Paying $100,000 cash gives you a 10 percent return on the money you've invested. Paying $2,500 down gives you almost a 50 percent return on the money you've invested. ($1,200 ÷ $2,500 = .48.) What bank, stock, bond, or mutual fund will pay you 48 percent?

Cash! Cash is not to be wasted. If you have $100,000 . . . you can buy not just one but many properties, including one *or more* priced at $100,000. Never be confused about the power of cash. And always use your cash wisely and make it work hard for you. Using it all in a single transaction can mean you won't be able to make an offer on another property. This is another reason to eliminate emotion from the decision-making arena.

You can give a seller the asking price, with little or no money down, and it will be far more profitable than if you were able to knock 10 percent off the asking price by putting up more cash up front. A personal comment: I love to give sellers their asking price. This eliminates the antagonisms that invariably pop up when the buyer tries to negotiate the lowest possible price and the seller thinks the buyer is looking for an unreasonable edge.

In fact, sometimes I'll even offer a premium *above* the asking price. We'll explore the benefit of this in the next chapter of this book.

And always remember, from this point forward: Net operating income, not gross income, determines the value of a property.

WATCH OUT FOR THESE:

Taxes are an "X-factor" in figuring net operating income. A tax assessor can increase the taxes when ownership changes hands, especially if the selling price is greater than the previous selling price . . . which happens more often than not.

Real estate taxes will generally average one to two percent of the total selling price, but don't guess at the amount. Rather, if you estimate net income based on what the taxes were last year, and the net seems thin, probably it will be even thinner.

You need to do some research, though. I've seen areas of the country where taxes approach 4 percent or more of the property's value.

And don't forget the number one cost of owning any property — maintenance. That's one reason you should establish a workable operating budget.

Expect unexpected nasty surprises. You don't know what they will be; you just know that sometimes they will be there. Allow for these when figuring whether or not you can expect a positive cash flow. *If you keep emotion out of the mix, your numbers will not only make sense; they'll be far more accurate.* So don't overestimate, nor underestimate, potential expenses. Overestimation can cause you to pass up a worthwhile investment; underestimation can cause you to lose money once you're the owner.

At worst you should have a break-even cash flow, but try to structure the terms of the purchase so you have a minimum $100 per month cash flow from each property or unit. Those are my own standards for properties I buy.

Add up all your expenses: Maintenance, taxes, insurance, and management. Does your income cover them *and* your debt service payments as well? If not, you will have a negative cash flow.

If you're buying a property that has existing tenants — that is, rental units, whether one or 200 — normally you can raise rents $15 to $20 a month without generating major move-outs. These are called "nuisance raises," and they can enhance your positive cash flow.

A guide, admittedly loose: For single family homes, your total expense figure, excluding management, will average 20 percent to 30 percent of effective gross income. (Total gross income less vacancy allowance equals effective gross income.) For multi-family properties — obviously, depending on the age and construction of the property and where it's located within the United States, your total expense figure will average 35 percent to 50 percent of effective gross income.

When you negotiate for rental properties, you should ask the sellers to show you their tax return. No, you don't want his or her complete personal income tax return; you want only the page whose figures reflect ownership and management of this property, their applicable Schedule "E."

For larger properties, a safe and very simple formula is to start with the gross income. Subtract the vacancy rate. (I typically use five percent for my area but that may be high or low in your area. Here's another example of where market knowledge becomes important.) Then subtract the expenses. The resulting number is, obviously, the net operating income.

An admonition: A "Bargain" property may not necessarily turn out to be a bargain. When you find a bargain-priced property, ask yourself the same dispassionate, emotion-free question you should ask with any transaction: "Can I afford the existing debt service, *plus* any new debt I'd be adding when I acquire it?" If the answer is no, you know what to do: Pass — or negotiate for a lower price and/or better terms.

Debt service includes existing mortgages whose payments you will take on and any mortgages you plan to put on the property. When you subtract this from the net operating income you can figure your cash flow. (Note: In real estate investing, cash flow is sometimes referred to as "cash throw-off.")

Let's suppose you set as a goal, for a property you plan to rent once you own it, a positive cash flow of $100 per month per unit. Do the simple arithmetic with various offers you might make and you'll quickly see whether you're going to clear $100 . . . or $50 . . . or $25 . . . or nothing. Then, without emotion, make a *businesslike* decision, about the offer you wish to make. Your decision might be to make an offer at the seller's asking price, but with a low interest mortgage to the seller. Or, perhaps you might choose to lease option the property. Or, if you have cash available, you might make a low all-cash offer. Regardless, at all times you will keep in mind your monthly cash flow objectives.

Don't be afraid to offer the seller's price, if all other elements and terms are in place. Trying to squeeze an extra
few thousand out of the deal may be a shrewd procedure
when you're ready to make a substantial cash down pay-

> I'm a drywall foreman, working for my dad's busi-
> ness. It's a very competitive business, and although our
> workload has gotten bigger, and clients have multi-
> plied, I really haven't gotten a raise in over 6 years.
>
> I bought your course about a year and a half ago,
> and since then have acquired 6 houses, a 5-unit build-
> ing, and two apartment complexes, with a total of 190
> units. My monthly positive cash flow is now $10,260. My
> wife, Perri, is still in shock. Our net worth is now $897,000.
>
> Now, my wife can stay home with our two young
> kids, plus there's money for vacations which wasn't
> there before. We've got retirement income, and
> money for our kids' educations. Your program has
> helped me look at life much more enthusiastically.
> Thank you, Carleton!
>
> — *Derek Brown, Washington*

ment, but it isn't so shrewd when you're trying to buy with no money down. The fellow with cash may possibly negotiate himself out of the deal because, even with $15,000 down, when he offers $10,000 less than you do with little or no money down, his offer may look worse.

One additional admonition: Beware of "Analysis Paralysis."

This is an ailment that afflicts many would-be real estate investors especially in the beginning. If you spend too much time analyzing and re-analyzing every property, you'll eventually reach a point at which you come to a dead stop. Analysis will replace action.

If you wait, wait, wait for the "perfect" investment, you may never become an investor. Don't let that happen. Make an offer based on the logical research you've completed. Analysis paralysis is really nothing more than fear. An absolute rule: Fear dissipates in direct ratio to the number of offers you make. And once you've closed two or three deals, you're a professional. Professionals are immune to analysis paralysis.

A QUICK EXAMPLE OF THE NO-MONEY-DOWN ADVANTAGE

Visualize two properties, identical in every respect. Each is priced at $100,000, and assume that's a fair price. One requires all cash at close. The other is available for no money down, with the seller carrying a low-interest mortgage for $100,000.

It's not even close. The better deal is obvious.

Let's be realistic. When a seller wants $100,000 cash, there is a reasonable likelihood that you can get the place for $80,000 to $90,000, if you pay all cash. When a seller is willing to carry the entire purchase price on a low-interest mortgage, there is a strong likelihood that *if you're lucky* (beating others to the opportunity) you can buy the property for $100,000. But, because of the terms, you may even be agreeable to paying $105,000 - $110,000. So the cash deal is better because you have a possible swing of $20,000 to $30,000, right?

Not necessarily.

I live and invest in the L.A. area. I've heard that some people think this is a tough market to make money in. They obviously have not benefitted from your instruction.

In the last year, I've bought seven single family homes using *none* of

my own money. And, by pulling cash out through refinances (they all still have positive cash flows), I've paid off over $100,000 of personal debt. Your system has saved my life and turned it around.

— *Ken Le Tourneau, California*

Compare having $100,000 cash versus having a house worth $100,000, free and clear. Which gives you greater latitude for swinging new deals? Obviously, the cash.

With $100,000 cash I can buy many homes, each of which might be worth $100,000 or more — $10,000 down here, $5,000 down there, no money down over there. The simple rule: *Cash is king.* Unless you have a great amount of it, use it as judiciously as you possibly can. If you have access to $100,000, and put it all in one property, you obviously are limiting yourself in future transactions. Granted, you will have $100,000 in equity in your property (and I have many low-cost and creative ways to take equity out that I'll introduce you to later) but why put all your "cash eggs" in one basket.

Cash is king and if you use it wisely, you can be the crown prince.

CHAPTER NINE

Teach Yourself to Think Creatively In Problem-Solving

(Suggestion: Knowledge is a wonderful substitute for dollars . . . but dollars aren't a wonderful substitute for knowledge. Don't assume profits are automatic because you've had one or two successful real estate transactions. Every deal is different. Every deal requires the application of knowledge — creative thinking — two principles that remain constant. Raw application of principles may bring occasional success but also may bring occasional failure. Adding creative thinking to these principles results in a potent mixture that makes ongoing success far more likely.)

THE POWER OF SELF-ESTEEM

A wise man said, "Once your mind is stretched by new ideas, it never can go back to its former size."

Every one of us is born with some creative talent. Obviously, some have a greater natural ability than others . . . just as some have a greater athletic talent or mechanical aptitude. But every human being has *some*.

What happens to it?

163

From childhood, our creative processes can be stifled by the ongoing admonition: "There's only one right answer to this question." Answers to questions . . . and problems . . . are black or white. No grays.

Most people are pressed into molds. The standard rule — no, *gospel* — is just that: Standard. "Be like everybody else." "Why are you such an oddball?" "Why don't you think like the rest of us do?" What these questions really mean is, "Why don't you run on tracks?" And sadly, most people do.

That's the advantage of being a real estate investor. The very nature of real estate investing is entrepreneurial — that is, you're in business for yourself. You're the decision-maker. You not only don't run on tracks, you can make money from those who do.

We're *forced* to stretch our minds. And once our minds are stretched by new ideas, they never can go back to their former size. That's why, today, I bless the day I was fired, back in 1970. I doubt that I'd still be working for someone else today, but that shock, that trauma, that apparent disaster forced me to become an entrepreneur considerably earlier than I otherwise would have.

No description I can give you is adequate to portray the excitement you will *feel* when you make your first real estate deal. It's *you*, not some company you represent. *You* solved problems creatively. *You* made decisions and implemented them. Your mind is stretched beyond its former limit. No going back! You'll never again settle for the "life of quiet desperation" so many others endure because they don't know about the wonderful world that exists outside their narrow sphere.

Watch. Your self-esteem will rise and rise and rise, as you take hold as a real estate investor. Self-esteem carries with it some valuable by-products . . . confidence; the ability to communicate; "position" within your social and business circles.

WHY TEACH YOURSELF CREATIVITY?

The very word "creativity" terrifies some people. They visualize mad-looking youths with headbands, reciting poetry by candle-light. They picture wild-eyed copywriters and artists at advertising agencies. They imagine paint-spattered "artists" whose canvases are smeared with meaningless lines and dots.

No, that's not what I mean when I say, "Teach yourself creativity," I'm using a far more practical interpretation of creativity: *Finding a new, different way to solve an old problem.* Easy? Simple? Yes, provided you understand what the problem is. If you're trying to buy a particular house, the problem isn't whether or not the house makes sense to you as an investment; we've passed that point. The creative problem is how to structure a transaction, at the end of which the house has changed hands, and you now own it.

TWO MENTAL EXERCISES

Believe it or not, you can exercise your mind to think creatively, just as you exercise your muscles to add strength and stamina. Two parallel exercises are involved.

I can describe the first creative exercise two ways. I might call it *neuro-linguistic programming* (which sounds like some scientific mumbo-jumbo) or I can state it clearly, by describing it as creating a positive state of mind. Same thing! You become — and I'm not joking — like the little engine in Walt Disney's cartoon: "I think I can, I think I can, I think I can" . . . and each time you repeat "I think I can" you move forward a little more. And after you've cleared the hump, it's "I knew I could, I knew I could, I knew I could."

You see, creativity is a state of mind. Do you know how many cells the typical brain has? Eighteen billion. That's a lot less than the national debt, but it's still a whole bunch of brain cells. They're sitting up there, waiting for you to give them directions so they can go to work. And they *will* believe whatever you tell them.

You know the old anecdote about the two people who saw a glass half-filled with water. One remarked, "The glass is half full." The other commented, "The glass is half empty." Which of the two would be more likely to be a success?

I'm perfectly aware that some who have read this far in this book have been saying to themselves, "Maybe some people can buy property with no money down, but I can't. I just can't bring myself to make an offer like that to a perfect stranger." If that's your attitude, *of course* you can't. You've uttered a self-fulfilling prophecy.

But if you say, "I think I can," and you make a commitment to learn the techniques and strategies (this book is a good start), then you're going to make some deals. Some of the most successful real estate investors I've met were so introverted they could barely tell me their names in seminars I conducted. What brought them to life? A light-bulb went off, illuminating eighteen billion brain cells: "I think I can. I knew I could."

The second exercise is a simple realization: You realize that every problem has many solutions. Does one plus one always equals two? No, it doesn't. Two people working together can accomplish more than two individuals working alone. We see on the news a group of bus passengers, working together, lifting the bus out of a mud-hole. If they worked as individuals that bus would sit there, stuck.

There is a parallel in investing. Once you become a real estate investor, your brain goes into overdrive. You begin to see multiple solutions to problems — "If this doesn't work out, we'll try that; if that doesn't work out, we'll try another

Since I've bought your course, I haven't quit buying property. I listen in when people talk about a property for sale and always find out who the owner is and if possible how to get in touch with that owner.

As you know, sometimes it doesn't work out. That's part of being a real estate investor. But when it does work out, it makes a person feel like he's accomplished something big. To date, I have bought over 1.25 *million* dollars worth of property, my latest being an eleven-plex. Total, on all the properties, I've put less than $6,000 down, and have $500,000 worth of equity.

I can be tough and I've learned to be inventive. I'm not afraid to wheel and deal; to haggle. In fact, I now like to create "unusual" offers. Most of all, I like to set my own technique on how to handle most of the deals. It is getting to be more fun all the time. We now are getting a loan from the bank to finance our new 3,000 square foot house and get to live some of my childhood dreams!

— John Firestine, Nebraska

solution." I personally am convinced that any problem has ten or a dozen solutions. All we have to do is think of them. And we have eighteen billion brain cells at our command.

One way of exercising is to use this approach on the very next problem that comes your way. Immediately, sit down with pen in hand. Write as many solutions as come to mind. Chances are that the first few times you do this, you'll come up with two or three and then have to ponder for a while to think of more. But as that mental muscle stretches, you'll find yourself coming up with five or six to begin with. And gradually, some ideas you've discarded because they seem outlandish won't seem outlandish at all, because you'll recognize them as potential solutions.

If you're serious about stretching your creative brain power, don't let yourself go away from this exercise in problem solving until you've listed ten solutions, even if it takes you several days. Do this and you'll find that each time you practice, less time is required.

A little rule that can be helpful not just in real estate but in every aspect of your life:

Just because a solution seems unusual, that alone is no reason to discard it.

A second rule that can stretch not just your mind but your entire future: Don't let being good at what you do stop you from being better. Complacency is the Number One saboteur of creative thinking . . . the Number One cause of a previously inventive entrepreneur slowly corroding to a "We've always done it this way" mentality.

An advantage — and it's a big one — of being able to think creatively, of being able to come up with multiple solutions to a problem, of avoiding the "We've always done it that way" mentality, of accepting rejection as part of the business, is that you won't have much competition when you're negotiating. Others may have more money. But you'll have the edge, because your "bag" of solutions will invariably include one that makes more sense to the seller. A win/win proposition for both of you.

CREATIVE PROBLEM SOLVING

You *know* you're a creative problem solver when you have problems. That's a given.

Here is what I mean by that: People who lack creativity accept what's dished out to them. While this is a generalization, it is basically that they accept the situation not as a problem, but as an uncontrollable circumstance. They recognize few problems because they never try to solve problems.

Creative people recognize problems . . . then decide on ways to solve those problems.

So creative people — people who do something — in a sense, have more problems than non-creative people — people who do nothing. I love to face problems and solve them. I wouldn't have it any other way, and I hope you wouldn't either.

And I certainly don't care whether, when I make an offer, it differs from the "norm." You shouldn't either. Here's what I mean: The beginner-investor too often accepts the concept that a "standard" way of paying money exists. That beginner (and some people remain beginners for all their professional lives) concludes if he or she can't meet the "standard" way of paying money, no deal can be struck.

Baloney!

You know by now: It's very possible that the buyer doesn't have to pay any money at all. What gives us an edge — you and me — as real estate investors is our creative problem solving. So a deal varies from "standard." So what? When buyer and seller agree on terms, the contract exists, whether it's standard or not.

In fact, for the astute real estate investor a "standard" deal can be very costly. Example:

A "standard" transaction might mean conventionally financing 70 percent to 80 percent of the purchase price through a bank or savings and loan. In addition to the loan itself, the buyer pays an application fee — which can be as high as $500. The buyer also pays "points" for the loan, and points can range from one percent to three percent. (Note: One point equals one percent of the loan amount.) Other origination fees and costs also may be involved. And all this is on top of the down payment of 20 percent to 30 percent and a high interest rate. Lots of cash!

Meanwhile, if a broker is involved, the seller is paying a 5 to 7 percent commission. All this money pours out from both sides in fees and expenses. It's "standard."

Now look at the same transaction with creative thinking behind it. The buyer assumes the seller's existing mortgage (or buys with a contract for deed) and gives a note to the seller for the difference. The buyer has no down payment, no financing fees, none of the holdups and slowdowns and money bleeding that attends standard transactions. And, the interest rate may be a lot lower.

The seller has a number of ways of converting the note to cash (some of which you'll learn later in this book) and pays no brokerage commission if you are buying from a "for sale by owner." Both parties benefit because they didn't turn-off their creativity.

We've touched on the dual purpose of this book. The first purpose, obviously, is to prepare you to negotiate without injecting emotion but with an open mind. The second purpose, not so obviously, is to prepare you with procedures and techniques that work, so you'll be prepared with many creative options as you negotiate.

Thomas Edison was asked how he could deal with 1200 failed experiments while trying to invent the incandescent light bulb. "Twelve hundred times you failed," he was chided. "No, I didn't," he answered. "I just found 1200 ways not to do it."

THE BENEFIT OF "TELL ME MORE"

We all tend to fire from the hip. We get partial information and draw a conclusion. We interrupt someone who's explaining a circumstance to us and toss out a reply — many times to our later regret. We form a hard opinion based on partial facts because we're impatient or, worse, because we *think* we have the whole package of information in hand.

Three little words can be invaluable in our determination to think creatively and our parallel determination to avoid a case of foot-in-mouth disease: *Tell me more.*

"Tell me more" is a wonderful substitute for "Here's what I think." Reliance on this little phrase will have us asking questions instead of drawing premature conclusions.

"Tell me more" becomes especially valuable when: a) an offer seems too good to be true, or b) when the answer seems too obvious. So a major rule I hope you'll observe from this point forward (and by the way, it also works in your personal life):

The key to creative problem solving is — ask questions. Don't draw conclusions.

You see the benefit of asking questions . . . and it's a primary benefit, not a secondary benefit . . . is that questions, and the answers to them, open up all sorts of possible solutions to a problem. And because a question automatically involves the person of whom the question is asked (a claim you can't make about opinions or statements that you make), the other party is more likely to share information that may lead to a variation from "standard."

For hundreds of years one of the basic principles of salesmanship has been, "Put yourself in the position of the other party to the transaction." This can be powerful when it relates to empathy, but this concept can be dangerous when it comes into conflict with creative thinking. We're likely to conclude, as we try to structure an offer: "What kind of seller would ever accept an offer like that?" Putting ourselves in the minds of someone else in that manner can destroy the confidence behind making an unorthodox offer which might otherwise be accepted if presented with confidence and logic.

Here's a fine example of creative thinking that made possible a transaction that never could have occurred if the buyer had said either "I don't see how I can do this" or "They'll never accept it." A couple lived in a mobile home. They decided they wanted to move to a more conventional home and would lease out their mobile home.

Just one problem: The mobile home park regulations permitted occupancy only by owners.

This was their creative solution to the problem, 180 degrees from standard: They found a renter and deeded a one percent ownership to him. That deed was recorded in the public records. To protect their own position, they received a Quit Claim Deed for that one percent back from the renter. They simply held that Quit Claim Deed until the tenant left, then they recorded it, restoring their 100 percent ownership and extinguishing the renter's legal interest. So they didn't circumvent the regulations of the mobile home park. They didn't use subterfuge. They applied creative thinking to the problem and accomplished a transaction that otherwise could not have occurred.

An example you might use as a template for one of your own forthcoming deals:

One of my "students" in Chicago wanted to buy a condominium the present occupant owned free and clear — no mortgage. The seller was willing to finance 50 percent of the purchase price. My student asked the bank for a 50 percent mortgage — very little compared with the usual 70 percent to 80 percent mortgage. The bank asked how much of his own cash he was putting into the property. He explained that the seller was accepting a mortgage that used another property he, the buyer, owned, for collateral and therefore he was not putting any cash into the transaction. The bank treated that as the equivalent of a cash down payment, and he bought the property with no money down.

(If that last paragraph doesn't come clear on the first reading, please re-read it until it does. It's a classic example of creative thinking; of pyramiding what you have to enable you to acquire what you otherwise couldn't get.)

A QUICK RECAPITULATION

The two exercises described earlier in this chapter can bring you wealth beyond any current hopes. Those two exercises are: a) creating a positive state of mind, a positive mental attitude, and b) developing the firm conviction that every problem has many solutions.

Your creative talent is already there in your mind. Exercise it and you'll reap benefits that those who aren't creative problem solvers never can match.

CHAPTER TEN

A Few of the Many "No Money Down" Buying Techniques

*(Suggestion: Creative financing isn't new. An organized, deliberate, win/win approach may be regarded as new, however, because too often a no-money-down offer has been designed to favor the buyer and even insult the seller. Change your thinking. A flexible, motivated seller can become your "partner" in structuring a deal that benefits everybody. This **very important** chapter offers a number of ways of making that partnership not only possible, but probable.)*

LEVERAGE . . . PROS AND CONS

Get your pencil and paper out. This chapter moves deep into the heart of techniques you should know if you're to be not only a serious real estate investor, but a successful real estate investor as well.

Some of these procedures are quite sophisticated. I advise against trying one you don't completely understand. You can get burned. I also advise studying each one until you do understand it. Once you have them all firmly planted in your mind, you are, indeed, well on your way to becoming a professional real estate investor.

You certainly have heard the term "creative financing" before you ever picked up this book. Creative financing has come to the aid of sophisticated investors for decades. Giant companies change hands through creative financing. What *we're* discussing is the use of creative financing to avoid the always-increasing cost of borrowing money the "standard" way — from banks and mortgage brokers and other lenders. We're discussing the use of creative financing to overcome mortgage payments that are simply unaffordable . . . to buy property despite having poor or nonexistent credit and/or little or no cash. *That's* creative financing!

The key term is *leverage.* **Leverage.** The definition of leverage, for our purposes: Getting a little to do a lot. And how do we do that? With the venerable three-letter saying, "OPM" — Other People's Money.

Every few weeks we see in the financial pages of our newspapers that this company or that one — sometimes multi-billion dollar enterprises — have changed hands through a "leveraged buy-out." This means the buyer has used leverage instead of their own cash to accomplish the transaction. The only major difference between the leveraged buyout of a huge corporate enterprise and a single-family home is the number of dollars. The concept is the same: Use other people's money.

What people? They might be other investors that you put into a "syndicate" to buy property. It's done all the time. It might be an arrangement with the seller, as we've already discussed so often in these pages, where the seller takes back a mortgage or deed of trust. It might be arranging to sell off part of the property or something on it such as trees or mineral rights. It might be a dedication of future rents. Or it might be assuming an existing mortgage. Or it might even mean obtaining a new mortgage from a conventional lender; however, instead of a 70 to 80 percent loan it may be one for 40 to 60 percent of the property's value. Whatever it is, it's *other* people's money. The next part of this chapter will list ten separate and distinct sources for creative financing.

I needn't point out that the ultimate use of OPM is a 100 percent leveraged purchase. This means other people's money pays for everything. It's a true, genuine, 24-karat no-money-down buy. (Better yet, sometimes you can even get cash back when you buy property. I teach you how to do that in my home study course.)

Let's look at an example of the power of OPM: Suppose you invest $10,000 as a down payment to buy a property. It generates a spendable cash flow of $5,000 a year. That means, through leverage, you've earned 50 percent on your investment — one-half the amount you invested. But if you were able to buy that same property with no money down, that $5,000 return wouldn't be just 50 percent. It would be *infinite* — beyond a specific reference, because you had put up no dollars at all to get that return.

TEN SIMPLE SOURCES FOR CREATIVE FINANCING

While there are probably an infinite number of sources of capital (money) that can be identified by a creative and fertile mind, I believe they can be distilled down to ten basic categories.

We've touched on some of these and will make additional references to them later. But here, conveniently listed, are the ten.

A more comprehensive and detailed discussion of each of these, with charted examples and discussions of legal ramifications, exists in my home study course, available from The Professional Education Institute. But you will gain an overview and a basic understanding of each from the discussion that follows.

Source 1: The seller

The seller is an obvious source for financing. It is the seller who can give a "yes" or "no" answer to the question, "Are you open to financing arrangements?" or "Are you willing to take a promissory note?" Even assuming debts the seller has, may be a possibility. For example, paying off a large medical or dental bill with your credit cards (after you attempt to discount them) can be very enticing to a cash-poor seller.

Source 2: The property itself

Every piece of property has worth. The value lies not only in the actual value of the house and lot, but possibly in other areas as well. As just mentioned, trees and mineral rights may have cash value. Too, a vacant lot next door or furniture in the property may provide a source for cash. I recall some years ago, when Donald Trump bought the famous Mar-a-Lago mansion in Palm Beach, complete with all the furnishings, for seven million dollars, he pointed out that the value of the antique furnishings and artwork alone were worth more than seven million dollars.

Source 3: Investors

You'll find that this source becomes easier and easier as you acquire more properties. In fact, once your friends and acquaintances see how you're amassing properties and perhaps re-selling them, they'll often volunteer: "Can we get in on your next deal and loan you the money you need?" Investors will frequently loan money to you for a good rate of return, perhaps even sharing in a portion of the profit upon resale of the property.

Source 4: Partners

This source is the first cousin of the third source. For starters, you have family. And, family or not, it won't just be loyalty that causes them to advance money; if they have foresight, they'll see the relative safety and potential of their investment. Over a period of time, you may have a dozen or more partnerships comprised of family members, friends, and business associates. Each partner will have put up cash in return for an equity position (ownership) in the property.

Source 5: Tenants

Tenants represent rents that will come due. As such, they represent an opportunity to pre-collect rents by offering a discount for prepayment. Leases often are bankable (i.e., you can borrow using them as collateral), especially with commercial or multi-dwelling properties. Also, the last month's rents and security deposits from tenants who live in the property you are purchasing may be used as a source of capital.

Source 6: Real estate agents and brokers

If you truly understand the previous chapter in which we discussed creative thinking, you'll understand how real estate agents and brokers can represent a source of creative financing: Use their fees and commissions as a down payment. You can offer them a delayed bonus amount, in exchange.

Source 7: Your own services and skills

Many properties you'll look at are those that don't interest conventional buyers and investors because they need maintenance or repairs. Sanding, painting, replacing — all these have a dollar value without having to put up actual dollars, and you or a partner may be able to convert services or skills to dollars by identifying and meeting these needs. Going one step further, your services or skills may fulfill a need the seller has. For example, if you are a dentist, you might offer free dental care for three years.

Source 8: Existing loans on the property

Assuming an existing loan, or even a group of loans, can be parallel to cash, especially for a motivated seller. You take over the loans; the seller no longer has to pay them. This is a cash outlay the seller can avoid, and meanwhile you own the property without having to come up with any "front money."

Source 9: Unsecured paper and secured paper on equities

This is perhaps the most complex of the ten "uncomplicated" sources . . . which means it's the one you might use when the others aren't available, if you have a property with equity. *Equity* is the actual value of an asset, *minus* any amount owed on it. So if you have a property that is worth $100,000 with a debt of $80,000, you have $20,000 in equity. That $20,000 can be pledged as collateral for an institutional or private loan to buy another property with no money down. Or, you could write a note secured by your equity, and give it to the seller as a down payment.

Source 10: Institutional lenders

Banks, savings & loans, finance companies — these people have money to lend. In fact, they make their money by loaning money, so when you can show them: a) minimal risk, which real estate represents because it always has value, and b) an ability to pay, they'll have a real interest. Of course, their willingness to loan money will depend on your credit and your track record in making timely payments on debt obligations you may have had in the past. Or, you may have a partner who has a large net worth, who would be willing to co-sign a loan with you. Any or all of these should result in willingness to advance enough money so you can acquire the property without using your own cash.

> *In my home study course I explore these avenues fully. But, as I said earlier, the purpose of including them here is to build your awareness that more than one source exists. Think creatively. Other people's money is available, in one form or another.*

OLD WIVES' TALES, FOLKLORE, AND FICTION

Let me expose you to three of the most common misconceptions about buying property with no money down.

We've already looked at one of the basic fears that seizes the novice investor — the fear of being turned down by a scornful seller who says, "You're not coming up with any cash, so I certainly won't consider this offer."

First of all, motivated sellers don't say this. A transferred homeowner who has to move . . . a homeowner who already has bought a new home and is making two mortgage payments . . . a couple getting a divorce (and sadly, this is happening with ever-greater frequency) . . . an estate . . . a homeowner who doesn't want to (or can't) make the monthly mortgage payments — any of these can be, and often are, *very* receptive to a creative no-money-down offer.

But beyond that, a greater misconception exists: That a no-money-down offer always means the seller gets no cash. Not so. Far from it. Many no-money-down techniques require no money from you but still put some cash in the seller's pocket. For instance: A circumstance in which the property's existing equity becomes the "down payment," with the seller getting part of that equity in cash.

Example: A seller's property is worth $100,000 and has a $30,000 mortgage. By obtaining a new mortgage for $60,000, the $30,000 mortgage could be paid off, leaving $30,000 in cash for the seller. The seller could then take the balance of his or her equity in a second mortgage or deed of trust for $40,000.

The point is that sometimes the seller *can* get cash . . . but it doesn't come out of *your* pocket.

A second bit of folklore is that the seller has to be "down and out" to be flexible. We've already covered this misconception and know that just doesn't have to be the case. In addition to the reasons for motivated sellers just described, another major one exists: Emotional dissatisfaction with a property. The seller just wants to get away. "No reasonable offer refused" doesn't have to mean the seller is on the rocks. It just as easily can mean the seller is — well, eager to sell. In my opinion, you'll encounter more of these than you will sellers who are down on their luck and you'll have an easier, faster time negotiating with them.

An excellent source for property is from older investors who want to retire. Often, they want to take novice investors "under their wing" and help them. It feels good. (I know; I've done it!)

The third misconception requires some thought to comprehend. It's a situation you might encounter in which a seller's back is against the wall. The seller wants to sell but also wants to walk away with some cash. They insist on this happening or "No deal."

Consider this though: Inflexibility is like flexibility. It isn't a permanent state of mind. A seller can look you in the eye and demand, "Come up with some cash if you want to buy this place." Your reply can be, "Here's my card. If you change your mind or want to open a discussion about some possibilities that can benefit both of us, give me a call. I'm interested and I'm ready to move fast." You'll never hear from some. But you *will* hear from others. Sellers' circumstances can change suddenly. "I can sell this place tomorrow" can change to "Where are the buyers" when a homeowner has to move and very badly wants to sell and no cash offers are on the table. Today's inflexible seller can be tomorrow's "Make me an offer" seller. Remember, too: You may have ways to give a seller cash at closing without coming up with the money yourself.

"NO MONEY DOWN" TECHNIQUES — SOME SIMPLE, SOME COMPLEX

This component and the next may be the most vital, most crucial, most significant of anything you'll see in this book. I suggest you mark this chapter and read it through at least three times.

A disclaimer: The examples I'll use are for illustrative purposes only. One of the wonders of real estate investing is that every deal is different. This is what keeps us alert, excited, and ahead of the plodders who look for sameness.

A second disclaimer: There is no way I can include in this book either the large number of "no money down" techniques, or the depth of discussion about each, that I present in my home study course manual and accompanying audio and videotapes. But I have no question that the techniques that follow will open your mind to a whole new world of creative finance. Will you be able to use the information that follows, in the marketplace? Absolutely! Can you buy property using the ideas presented? You bet! But if you really want the "whole ball of wax," as my mother used to say . . . stay tuned.

> *As you evaluate these techniques, keep in mind a basic premise of real estate investing: Rental rates usually are commensurate with value AND they usually go up.*

Technique #1: The wrap-around mortgage

Let's use an example to clarify the meaning and benefit of a wrap-around mortgage.

Suppose a seller's property has a fair market value of $50,000. It has an existing assumable $30,000 first mortgage at 8 percent interest. Payments are $245 per month. With that $30,000 mortgage, the seller's equity is $20,000 — the value of the property, minus the mortgage.

You could make a simple no-money-down offer — assume the $30,000 mortgage and give the seller a second mortgage for $20,000 at, say, nine percent interest. Your total payments for the two mortgages might be $445 per month. But you may have a better way, avoiding the fees and costs of assuming that first mortgage.

Offer the seller a total "wraparound" mortgage for the entire $50,000, with an interest rate of nine percent and a term of 20 years. (In some states this type of mortgage is known as an A.I.T.D., an "All Inclusive Trust Deed.") You'd agree to make payments *directly to the seller* of $450 per month, approximately the same amount you'd pay on the first and second mortgages. The seller continues to pay on the original first mortgage, which you *don't* assume. See what happens? Your new mortgage literally "wraps" around the existing mortgage.

Everybody benefits. The seller is making one percent on the first mortgage amount (he is paying eight percent and

> When I got your course, I had about $5,000 to my name, and $10,000 per *month* of bills (a real negative cash flow). Now, I'm making over $100,000 of spendable cash flow per year from my real estate and have a net worth (liquid) of over $600,000! My office is my home (which is free and clear) and my life is much more relaxed. I've done pretty much all of this using only one of your techniques — lease options.
>
> I love using the "Sandwich Lease" and have received many thank you notes from people I've put into my homes who never would have been able to own a home otherwise. I thank the Lord, and Carleton Sheets, for making this course.
>
> — *Joe DeRosa, Colorado*

you are paying nine percent), and he gets a fairly high rate of interest on his equity (the $20,000) — considerably more than he could get from a certificate of deposit or savings account. His equity is constantly growing, because his first mortgage is being paid off at a much faster rate than the wraparound mortgage. You benefit because you have the property with no money down and none of the closing costs and fees.

Technique #2: Using equity in one property to buy another

This is one of the simplest of the techniques, mentioned before in this text. What do you own, in which you have equity? A home? A boat? An investment property? An automobile? A diamond ring? A lot? A time share? Whatever it is, use that equity or the actual asset itself as a down payment on another property you're buying.

Obviously, this technique is available only if you do have an equity in some kind of property.

An example of this technique: You're buying a two-family building that's offered at $60,000. The existing mortgage is $25,000, so the seller's equity is $35,000 — the difference between the offering price of the property and the mortgage.

You offer a promissory note for $15,000, backed by the equity in one of your assets. Or, you offer to "give" the seller your $15,000 travel trailer or diamond ring or time share. That note or asset becomes the "down payment." You ask the seller to agree to either a $20,000 second mortgage or a $45,000 "Wrap Around Mortgage"($25,000 existing first mortgage plus $20,000 for the equity. See Technique number 1.)

See what happens? The moment you close, you immediately have $15,000 in equity in the new building. Where does it come from? The $15,000 second mortgage or asset you've used as a down payment.

In March I borrowed $18,800 off my first property to purchase a house that had been heavily damaged by fire. I spent $18,500 of this money to purchase and re-build the house. I then rented the house for $400 per month. Six months later, I borrowed $28,605 on this property to buy two more houses. One now rents for $395 monthly giving me a $205 monthly profit after the mortgage payments. The other profited me $25,000. I paid $24,750 for it and it was appraised at $49,900. It rents for $400 monthly which is all profit. I then bought a house for $13,500, spent two weeks remodeling it at a cost of $1,400, and now rent it out for $395 per month. It is appraised at $31,000. I used the creative method Carleton describes in his course of buying one property for cash, refinancing, and buying the next one, etc.

I plan to own at least 15 properties and have them paid for in the next 10 years so that I can have a retire-ment fund of at least $72,000 a year. I am well on my way to attaining my goal.

— *Stanley B. Landers, Georgia*

If the seller says, "I positively have to come out of this with some cash," The seller can sell your promissory note to a third party, who may discount the amount somewhat, but the seller will still receive cash.

Technique #3: Land Contracts or Agreements for Deed or Contracts for Deed (They're All The Same Animal)

Buying "on contract" is common and popular in some parts of the United States and barely heard of in others. Frequently, buyers use it to acquire vacant land, but it works for improved real estate as well.

Compared with some of the techniques we've investigated and explained, this one is deceptively simple: The buyer doesn't get a deed until a stipulated number of payments have been made. No mortgage is involved. The buyer has a contract. When the required number of payments stipulated in that contract have been made, he gets the deed. At that point, he will have sufficient equity to obtain a mortgage or the seller will carry the financing.

Buying on contract is a "natural" no-money-down transaction. But a warning: If the Contract for Deed extends for some years, natural disasters and unanticipated uninsured losses can wipe out all the payments you've made. Protect yourself in the contract, at least to the extent that a) the seller warrants that he/she has clear title, and b) you carry adequate insurance to protect your interest against any loss. You also should, if possible, make your monthly payments to a title company, or trusted third party, who in turn would make monthly payments due on any underlying mortgages the seller has on the property.

If you enter into an Agreement for Deed, be sure to record the agreement in your county courthouse.

Technique #4: Borrow the broker's commission

Sometimes when a property listed by a broker requires just 10 percent down, the reality behind that situation is a desire on the part of the seller to just receive enough cash at close to cover the broker's commission and closing costs.

As you know, typical broker commissions range from 5 percent to 7 percent. If one broker both lists the property and sells it, he or she gets it all; if one broker lists the property and another sells it, the two brokers split the commission.

For a real estate investor, the best opportunity for negotiating to "borrow" the commission lies in approaching the listing broker. That way, the listing broker will also be the selling broker and will receive 100 percent of the commission. Brokers may be reluctant to consider delaying receipt of their commission, but that reluctance can be tempered by an offer in which you give the broker a note for an amount higher than the commission — for example, $3,500 for a $3,000 commission.

Another way to overcome their reluctance is to subtly tell him you are considering going to a friend who's an agent (don't we all have friends who are agents?) because that friend will agree to take his or her share (50 percent of the commission) in the form of a note. So, Mr. Broker, here's the choice: "Either take all of your commission in the form of a note, or only get half of it in cash. What do you think?"

Technique #5: Deposits, rent credits, and real estate tax credits

When you close on a property, you get a credit for unpaid real estate taxes. If it's rental property, you will also get a credit for prepaid rents, security deposits, and a percentage of rents paid in advance for the month in which you close.

The amount can be considerable and also is instantly available, because you, as the new owner, have no expenses for the first month. Your taxes may not be due until the year's end, and mortgage payments and utility bills aren't due until the following month. You can use the following month's rents to make your first mortgage payment.

Technique #6: A True Zero-Interest, Little Or No Money Down Technique: Lease Options

In some ways, I might be accused of saving the best for last. (My mother used to say, "Save the cream in the Oreo cookie for last. You'll enjoy it more.") Because there are so many variations of this technique, it truly is more of a strategy, but here's how it works.

The seller gives you the right to purchase his or her property: a) at a predetermined price or formula for price and b) for a specific period of time. When this occurs, the seller is known as the optionor and the buyer is known as the optionee. The seller is bound by the contract or agreement, but you, the buyer, are not. You can walk away at any time.

Because of the apparent "one-sidedness" of this contract, it would seem to benefit only you, the buyer. Not so, as you'll see in a moment.

Let's look at an example: Assume a seller has a home for sale for $80,000. You may have seen the home advertised either in the "For Sale" or "For Lease" columns (or both) in the classified ads section of your local newspaper. The ad said, "Seller will lease-option" or "Rent To Own". Or, maybe the seller never even considered lease optioning the property until you suggested it and got his attention.

Here's what the seller may want. He will sell for $80,000 or give you a one year lease option on the property for the same amount with rent of $800 per month. Each month, $50 of the rent will be credited towards the purchase price. You can live in the property or lease it out, but that one year, he tells you, will give you time to save some money and get your credit in order. This is a typical but very unappealing proposition on the seller's part.

Here's what you will propose: "I'll give you $80,000 for the property (you may want to start at $70-$75,000, but may ultimately be willing to pay $85,000 — stay tuned) on a 5-year lease option (settle for 3 if you have to, but no less) under these terms: "I'll pay you more than the market rent rate of $800 per month. I'll go $900, but in return I want 50 percent or $450 a month credited toward the purchase price." Negotiate the terms. Don't be timid.

Would a seller have to be crazy to do this? No! Remember, I said there are benefits for both the seller and the buyer. Let's look at the seller's benefits:

- He is (potentially) getting his asking price, maybe more
- He is getting a premium rent, of which only $450 has to be reported as income before the option is exercised
- He has a stable tenant who will pay on time (or the option will be lost)
- The tenant (optionee) will take good care of the property
- If the option is not exercised, it is forfeited and the seller has received far more rent than the market would otherwise bring
- Any option money or consideration received on the front-end is forfeited if the option is not exercised

Now, look at your benefits as the buyer (optionee):

- There is an excellent chance the property will appreciate over the 3 years, beyond the contract price
- While you are paying a premium rent, you are getting a 50 percent credit toward the purchase price, in this case, $16,200 ($450 × 12 × 3) over 3 years
- If you can rent the property for $900 per month, your payment is covered. If you can only get $800 per month, the $100 per month negative cash flow you'll experience is small compared to the $450 a month savings (credit towards the purchase price you are receiving)
- At the end of 3 years, an 80 percent bank loan would cover the amount needed to buy the property, so the purchase will be no money down
- At the end of 3 years, if you don't want to buy the property, you WON'T walk away. Why? You can sell your option. Will it be worth $16,200 plus any option consideration you had paid? Maybe. Will it be worth $1? Of course. Can you get $10,000? Probably.

You can see that, with the rent credit that applies to the purchase price, the seller is effectively financing this portion at zero interest. And if the security deposit and the first and last month's rent from a tenant equal or exceeds the option consideration required, "Shazam", we have a 24 kt. zero interest no money down deal.

Are you ready for this? It works with apartment buildings and commercial buildings and even businesses. And, if you have a dead asset, like an old car or a time share, that could be used as the option consideration at a value that is negotiated between you and the seller, and of course would apply toward the purchase price.

Technique #7: Using discounted bonds

This is just one of several techniques that are kind of exotic. Yet, this marvelous technique is relatively uncomplicated. It's one of my personal favorites.

The seller may be willing to help with the financing; but some sort of collateral is necessary. How about good (not "junk") bonds? They're incredibly credible.

The best candidates for this technique are zero-interest tax-free bonds such as those issued by municipalities or counties. However, if the seller is in a low tax bracket, then taxable bonds may work even better.

As you acquire the property, you obtain a new mortgage. Part of the money pays off the old mortgage, part goes to the seller, and part buys tax-free bonds, which you will use to collateralize a *note* to the seller.

You may have to make interest payments until the bonds mature, but when they do they represent a burst of cash. You'll have a problem only if your budget is faulty.

These bonds can be bought for a fraction of their face value — for example, $500 for a $1,000 bond due ten or more years later. If a $100,000 property has an existing $25,000 mortgage (the mortgage should be less than 30 percent of the property's value for this technique to work best), then you could put a new $65,000 first mortgage on the property. After you pay off the existing $25,000 mortgage, the remaining $40,000 could be used this way: $35,000 would be used to buy $70,000 worth of bonds, and the balance of $5,000 would be given to the seller in cash.

You can see that, if the first mortgage is small enough, you could even put cash in your pocket with this technique!

And, if you are trying to sell a property, simply make the terms more "seller-friendly" and sell your property immediately, to all those credit-poor, cash-poor people who desperately want to own their own home and can't qualify or buy any other way.

GOVERNMENT AID AND OTHER POSSIBILITIES

We've touched on many ways to buy property for no money down. In addition, the federal government has a whole group of federal loan guarantee programs on which you might be able to lean, ranging from loans for condominium units to loans for the elderly to loans for manufactured home parks. Look into these. You never know when one is *the* just-right one. The Professional Education Institute has a video specifically covering these opportunities. Call them if you're interested. And, as you can imagine, there is a considerable amount of information on this subject in my home study course.

Are you thoroughly confused by the plethora of available ways to buy property for no money down? Wonderful! That's a whole lot better than not being confused because only one way exists.

The techniques just discussed can be, and often are, an important part of the arsenal of a successful real estate investor. Don't think that they are the only methods, however.

As I mentioned earlier, I can't present an exhaustive analysis of all of them in this book. If you want comprehensive coverage, I suggest you contact the Professional Education Institute to gain access to my home study course. There you'll find a comprehensive in-depth analysis of these techniques and strategies (and more, including a whole expanded section on options, in print, audio, and video formats).

The more you understand about all the possibilities that may be open to you, the more success you'll have acquiring property with no down payment.

This chapter is unquestionably the most technical, most complicated, and potentially the most perplexing chapter in this book. Don't let complication stand in the way of getting you started in real estate. While I suggest that you read it over and over and over, because it is, ultimately, the most rewarding chapter, don't let it breed inertia. At some point you have to stop sharpening your axe and start chopping wood.

CHAPTER ELEVEN

How to Negotiate with Power

(Suggestion: From this moment until forever, erase from your mind the idea that a successful business person is one who bullies associates, is addicted to four-letter words, and feels the only way to convince people how much power is in his or her hands is to threaten and intimidate. From this moment on, keep that magical word **rapport** *uppermost in your mind in your dealings with people. Aside from the loyalties rapport will bring you, it also will bestow a far more valuable gift: Peace of mind.)*

TRUST AND CREDIBILITY — TWO POWERFUL ASSETS!

Logic says you can't negotiate with a loaded gun in your hand. The other party will either agree under duress, then quickly change his mind as soon as you leave . . . or take out his own gun, which might be bigger than yours . . . or just walk away, knowing your gun is loaded with blanks.

Logic also says you, I, and almost everyone else won't do business with a person they don't trust.

And logic says it's good business practice to enter the negotiating arena honorably and with open hands. If you *ever* want to do business with that individual again, trust and credibility are far more potent weapons than deception and duplicity.

So how do you convince a seller that you're "on the up-and-up"? How do you establish that magical relationship based on rapport? How do you generate a state of mind in which the other party thinks, "I trust this guy"?

Some procedures are psychological. Some are mechanical.

One of the easier mechanical procedures is to teach yourself to ask for and remember the other party's name. Over the phone, it's easy: You just jot it down when the other person mentions it. Don't be afraid to ask for spelling if it's an unusual name. (If you send a fax or letter to a seller and misspell his or her name, your chance of making a deal is somewhat reduced.)

Then use the name in conversations. It isn't "I'll tell you what," it's "I'll tell you what, Joe."

Another mechanical procedure is one a lot of people have trouble learning. It's this: Be a good listener.

We all like to talk. We all develop the habit of interrupting the other party so we can inject our own brilliant thoughts. You know what? If you can suppress that instinct, you'll learn a lot more and have far more ammunition for the eventual negotiating that takes place. You may have heard the old but always pertinent verse that first appeared in the now-defunct magazine *Punch* in 1875 . . .

> *There was an old owl, lived in an oak.*
> *The more he heard, the less he spoke.*
> *The less he spoke, the more he heard.*
> *O, if men were all like that wise bird!*

Listening gives you another advantage. You'll get a free education about the seller — what his/her interests are, what his/her hopes and fears are. Best of all, you'll get information about the property you never could hope to get in a formal arm's-length negotiation.

> I've been a real estate investor for several years. I sure wish Carleton's course was available when I first started investing. There's some great information in there that even a seasoned investor like me can pick up — tips on negotiating, taking cash out at closing. There's a lot of money to be made in real estate, and you don't have to learn the hard way how to do it. By the way, mostly because I got your course (to get me going strong) my net worth is now over $1 million, and I make $3,500 every month just from my rental properties.
> — *Bernie Jueden, Oregon*

Here's where psychology enters the picture: Be sincere. Don't just put on an act. Empathize with the seller. Some whom you'll come across are selling the home in which they grew up or have lived in for an extended period of time. They have an emotional attachment. Share that at-tachment. Understand their motivations. Put yourself in their shoes. They quickly will sense that your interest isn't the interest of someone trying to take advantage of them but the interest of a person who genuinely cares about what they think and feel.

THE GENTLE ART
OF DIPLOMACY

Let's suppose you've already visited the property, per-haps with a broker, or maybe viewed the property from your car. Ask to see it again, this time with the owner present. When a seller gives you a personal tour, your rela-tionship can move a long stride, from that of strangers to potential business associates. Strangers can't have rapport; business associates can.

But beyond that, your initial visit to the property can't have given you the in-depth knowledge you're about to re-ceive. You'll see aspects you missed. And you undoubtedly will have developed questions the seller can (and should) answer. Bringing up those questions when the two of you are together, especially if the questions are of a critical na-ture, is far less likely to breed antagonism and distancing than asking the questions over the telephone.

To this day I remember dealing with a buyer, when I was selling a piece of property I owned. I had it on the mar-ket for $215,000.

The fellow's belligerence was apparent from the moment we met on the property. He literally "sniffed" at each room and at the grounds; it was like a military in-spection, looking for something to criticize. He turned to me and said, "This property is not worth one penny over $180,000."

Stop for a moment. Put yourself in that buyer's position. If you wanted to buy the place for $180,000, how would *you* have worded this statement?

To me, the approach was a complete turnoff. I might have been willing to sell for $180,000, but not to that guy.

So how would you have worded it?

As a serious real estate investor with a carefully-cultivated sense of diplomacy, you probably would have said something like this: "You have a lovely property, and I think it's fairly priced. But I don't know that my budget can afford your asking price. I wonder . . . would you ever give some thought to a quick sale of $180,000. I'd love to be able to own this place." You see how you're blaming your lower price on someone or something else — in this case, your budget.

A valuable rule to follow is to avoid being overly critical of the property; and never be critical of the seller. You'll seldom, if ever, force the seller into lowering the price or terms by harsh criticism; you'll often get the seller to lower the price or terms by compliments and praises for those elements deserving compliments and praises, intermixed with soft critiques of those elements whose flaws are apparent.

That's the difference between a bully and a diplomat. Bullies have a hard time in real estate investing, because when their competitor is a diplomat, they invariably come in second.

Before you draw the conclusion that I'm endorsing a "Goody Two-Shoes" position, understand this: Don't let your sense of diplomacy cause you to deliberately overlook the faults of a property. That isn't diplomacy; it's naivete. Mentioning the property's weaknesses in a non-judgmental way can actually enhance rapport and get the seller to "open up" with information you otherwise might never get.

Additionally, this approach can be a help when you make an offer below the asking price, because the seller may better understand that your lower offer is based on the property and not just on a desire to drive down the price.

As is true of almost every aspect of a buyer-seller negotiation (or any other personal relationship, for that matter), if you try to visualize yourself in the other person's position considering how you would react to a statement, the possibility of rapport goes up enormously.

THE DIFFERENCE BETWEEN *WANTS* AND *NEEDS*

Is there a difference between a seller's *wants* and a seller's *needs?* Absolutely. A seller usually pays more attention to his wants than to his needs. (That may be why so many homes have four television sets and one bathtub.)

And *wants* are all the buyer usually learns about the seller: The asking price and the Terms. These *wants* may not at all match the seller's *needs.*

So, establishing rapport with a flexible seller may get that person to open up a little so you can find out why he or she is eager to sell. You aren't prying, you're fact-finding . . . while a direct question — "What do you plan to do with the money? — can generate a fast "None of your business." It also can generate, "Why do you want to know?" You have a ready answer: "I'm trying to structure a deal that will work for both of us and give you the cash you want" (need!).

Example: Suppose the seller says he needs all cash. Asking, diplomatically, what he plans to do with all that cash may well bring the answer, "To buy another house." This answer can serve you well, because it gives you the opportunity to explain some creative financing techniques that, by enabling the seller to buy a new home for little or no money down, will in turn make it easier for you to buy their home for little or no money down.

Knowing what the seller plans to do with the money can open avenues for you. I once had a seller who, after rapport had been established, told me he wanted a certain amount of cash right now so he could return to his native country, Greece, together with his furniture. I asked him if I could pay for his airline ticket and the cost of shipping the furniture as part of the closing, by charging both to my credit card. He was agreeable. The result of the negotiations allowed a nothing down purchase.

Regardless of the size of the deal — whether it's a three-bedroom house or a big apartment building — juggle these six variables as you negotiate: (Since they almost always are present, I call them the "invariable variables.")

1. Price (obviously)
2. Terms (interest rate, amount and length of mortgage)
3. Closing date
4. Amount of down payment
5. Amount of monthly payment
6. Property to be left, such as appliances

You can see: There are six separate areas in which you can negotiate. Since these areas almost always exist, why not pursue each of them? You may not be able to influence them all, but you have an excellent possibility of connecting with one or more, in a way that will be very favorable to you.

WHEN THE SELLER NEEDS AN EDUCATION . . .

A surprisingly large (or perhaps it's not so surprising) number of sellers won't understand the principles of crea-

> *This chapter deals with the psychology of negotiating. This concept fits very well because it represents the best way to make a dynamic point without generating antagonism or disagreement:*
> *Tell a third-party story. It isn't, "Here's what I've done before," but "Here's what a fellow on the South Side of town did."*
> *Be a story-teller, not a preacher!*

tive financing . . . until and unless you explain those principles to them.

Using the third-person approach can sidestep a confrontation in which the seller makes a flat statement with which you disagree. For example . . .

Suppose the seller says, "You see that house down the street? It sold for $100,000, and mine is a much better house than that one."

You've researched the neighborhood, as an astute real estate investor does. You could say, "You're wrong. I happen to know the house sold for only $85,000, and besides, it's nicer than yours." And, of course, you'll blow the deal.

Instead, shift to the third-party mode: "Yeah, I also had heard it sold for $100,000. But you know what, Tom? I was talking to a broker the other day and found out it sold for $85,000." (Note: Don't say, *"only* $85,000," which rubs the seller's nose in the difference, but plain, unadorned "$85,000.")

You've made your point without causing the seller to feel you're bullying or trying to out-smart him.

The point: Don't imply that you're smarter than the other party to the negotiation. You won't win a friend that way.

So starting a counter-argument with, "You know, I always believed the same thing, but you know what? . . ." can be a positive negotiating ploy.

WHEN TO MAKE A VERBAL OFFER AND WHEN TO MAKE A WRITTEN OFFER

Two aspects of Planet Earth are finite . . . that is, there's no way to change them. One is the amount of land (except for filling in waterfronts). The other is time.

Your time is an asset. Typing up or handwriting an offer, a legal document, takes time. So limiting yourself to formal written offers can be a hindrance to both your business tempo and to your enthusiasm.

You've tortuously (yes, painfully) prepared an offer to buy. While you were preparing it you made changes and alterations, trying to make it perfect for the seller and for you. The seller turns it down. You curse yourself for having wasted 45 minutes to an hour.

Had you, instead, made a verbal offer, confirming the offer with a handwritten note on the back of your business card — "Would be interested in a lease option at approximately $85,000. Call me if you're interested" — you'd have cut as much as an hour from the time you invested in the offer.

The legendary movie producer Samuel Goldwyn, as well known for his malapropisms (unintentionally humorous misuse of words) as well as for his films, is credited with this one: "A verbal contract isn't worth the paper it's written on."

True. It isn't worth the paper it *isn't* written on. But it's knowledge that can work for us just as much as it works against us. We all know the difference between making a direct offer to a seller and working through a broker. A broker cannot be forced to submit a *verbal* offer. The "submit any and all offers" doesn't include verbal offers because verbal offers aren't considered full-fledged legal offers.

But if I'm working directly with a seller, after having said the mandatory *(note, please!)* "I have no problem with your asking price. It's my budget I'm having a problem with." (As I said earlier, blame the differential on something other than the asking price.) I then will suggest an approximate price I'm willing to pay.

Then I'll say, "Let me leave you my card. If you ever see your way clear to considering something in my price range, give me a call." And I'll write the figure on the back.

That figure becomes the "bird in the hand."

Scribbling on the back of a business card isn't good business form if you're dealing with a broker. However, as an alternative — midway between a note on your card and a formal written offer — consider a letter of intent.

A letter of intent straddles the approach. It's informal; not a binding offer. It indicates, though, your good faith desire to acquire the property and, if the response is positive, it becomes a blueprint for a more detailed written offer.

The letter of intent doesn't specify *how* you propose to pay for the property. That isn't the purpose of this letter. It's a door-opener, not a substitute for a contract. The purpose is to find out whether you and the seller have any common ground.

Being too specific with terms in a letter of intent can damage the possibility of entering into a negotiation with the seller.

A tip: Try to include a complimentary statement about the property in your letter of intent.

Is the seller bound — or, for that matter, are *you* bound, if the seller accepts your letter of intent? No, the letter should clearly state; "Please understand that this is merely an expression of intent and *not a contract*. Neither party is bound to perform under the terms of this letter." Yes, I know this is formal wording for an informal letter; but you want to make it clear that all the parties are agreeing to do is get together to see whether both parties can agree.

Why do you *not* want the letter to be binding?

It's because you want to leave yourself room to negotiate, not only on the price but on the terms of the down payment, any seller financing, personal property that will be included, the closing date, and so forth. You may even decide to negotiate to purchase the property under the terms of a lease option.

As an aside, there's nothing wrong with your using a letter of intent when you're the seller, not the buyer.

Incidentally, when you find yourself making lots of offers, and you will be, you may find it helpful to have my contract on a computer disk so you can customize each one and print it right out on your printer. It's neat and professional. Contact the Professional Education Institute to obtain my "Real Estate Computer Toolkit," which has all my forms on it, as well as the financial calculator functions you'll need when doing "what if" scenarios for multiple offers.

PRESENTING THE MULTIPLE OFFER AND NONESSENTIAL CONTINGENCIES

Sometimes, when you determine that the seller may be willing to negotiate on the price, or terms, or both, you might present *multiple* offers — offers structured two or three different ways. (Be sure you'd be satisfied with whichever of the offers the seller expresses an interest in.)

You'd write a letter of intent in which you outline options: "I'd be willing to buy your property under any of these scenarios." Example (with a home offered for $100,000):

"Number one: I'd be willing to pay you $75,000 cash, closing in five days. Or, number two: I'd be willing to buy your property with $10,000 down, spread over a short period of time, with you holding financing at a market rate of interest, for $90,000. Or, number three: I'd pay $105,000 provided you give me 100 percent seller financing with monthly payments that would correspond with the cash flow from the property."

You've presented three options. And, you try to skew the results with the numbers you use. For example, you may be unable or unprepared to pay all cash, so you make your all cash offer so low that it's unlikely to be accepted. (Note: Even if it is the seller's choice, you're not legally committed to buy the property for all cash . . . although if it's a "steal" you may somehow find the cash needed.)

Multiple offers work. You've seen this concept in a more primitive use when a salesperson asks you, "Which one do you like better, the red one or the blue one?" instead of "Are you interested?"

Warning: Don't let the seller "cherry pick" a bit of one offer and a bit of another, such as the higher price and all cash. Explain that you've thought this through and each offer stands on its own as one you can afford to make.

I've become so convinced that multiple offers are the best way to approach buying a property that I now present only multiple offers in my letters of intent. Multiple offers force the seller to consider alternatives and seldom are rejected out of hand.

Another negotiating tool is the "nonessential contingency." Here's what that means:

If you agree that the smart negotiator gives something to get something, you will also agree that the smart negotiator asks for concessions. You may not need (or even

Before I bought your course, I was a self-taught real estate investor. I did most of my learning by trial and error, and ended up losing a lot of money in the process. It left me very frustrated.

Your course has so much good information in it! I picked up many, many ideas and techniques — things that I didn't know before, and some that I never would have thought of. It got me so motivated! Since buying your course, I have more than quadrupled the rental property I own, and increased my positive cash flow to over $70,000 a year! I even received a check for $93,000 when I refinanced one of my properties.

I now have the peace of mind that I've always wanted about my family's financial future, and my kids' education. We've got a nice house, and I don't worry about taking a long vacation, or a few days off from work to spend on a family outing.

I've dabbled in some other business-opportunities-from-home programs, and I would have to say that none have given me the return on my time, and investment, like real estate.

I wish I would have ordered your course sooner.

— *Phil Thompson, Tennessee*

want) these concessions. This means you're willing to readily give them up . . . in exchange for something you really do want.

While you probably can come up with hundreds of nonessential contingencies, here are five examples that you might use as negotiating pawns. You'll give them up . . . in exchange for getting an *essential* you really do want.

1. Longer amortization of a mortgage the seller will hold — say, 40 years instead of 30 years.
2. Seller pays all the closing costs instead of just part of the closing costs.
3. Seller gives a one-year warranty on all appliances.
4. Seller repaints the exterior and/or interior.
5. Seller leaves drapes and/or carpets and/or one or more pieces of furniture.

So you give in on one of these . . . or two of these . . . or all. So what? Each concession suggests a parallel concession by the other party.

CAUTION: Be cool. Don't present any of these nonessential contingencies as a demand.

THE ADVANTAGE OF A "NET/NET" PURCHASE

When the seller has a very small equity in the property, a "net/net" offer can be extraordinarily effective. "Net/net" means the seller walks away with a "net" cash amount. The buyer pays all the closing costs and transfer fees and title insurance and broker commissions and inspections and whatever.

Thus the seller knows that whatever the amount of cash is, it's *net.* Nothing comes out of it. They're going to get it all.

Are you wondering what advantage that may be to you? Actually, there are three separate advantages:

1. The brokerage commission, if a broker is involved, is calculated on a lower selling price.
2. If the broker is willing to take the commission in the form of a note, you need less cash.
3. It's entirely possible the actual mortgage will be less than the estimated mortgage. The sole beneficiary of this difference is you, the buyer. If it is more, the contract should call for the seller to accept a reduction in the net amount due by the amount of the difference.

The net/net concept is another one of those sophisticated "upgrades" you might want to try when you're more comfortable with your role as real estate investor. My home study course covers this in greater detail . . . so if you're interested in exploring this creative byway, you might want to make the nominal investment in the course. I say nominal because I've been told by so many students that they have saved thousands of dollars, often tens of thousands of dollars, as a result of my home study course, in buying a property. I've always thought if I could spend a penny to make a dollar, that's good sense. (My grandfather would have said that's a 100 percent profit.)

A VALUABLE NEGOTIATION CHECKLIST

Mark this page, because you'll enjoy better success, make more deals, and pocket more money by having this list of 22 potent points at hand . . . and going over each of them, point by point, before making an offer.

Try it. You'll like it. So will your bank account.

1. Deal as often as you can with two types of sellers: flexible sellers and sellers whose properties have favorable existing financing.
2. Establish both credibility and that marvelous word *rapport* with the seller.
3. Try to have all the owners there when you present an offer.
4. Present your offer in person, not over the phone.
5. Be sure all final offers are in writing.
6. Don't be hypercritical of the property, and don't ever criticize the seller. Be a diplomat.
7. In your conversations, don't use formidable words people fear. It isn't a "contract"; it's "paperwork."
8. Present your offer from the bottom up. This means discussing contingencies *before* mentioning your offering price. Don't let yourself get derailed on this.
9. Always make offers with *uneven* figures. This is a psychological ploy — the seller may think you have a specific reason based on your own research. So offer 8.7 percent, not 9 percent; offer $86,700, not $87,000.
10. If you're offering a low interest rate, offer it in dollars rather than percents. $150 per quarter on a $10,000 mortgage seems to be more than six percent interest.
11. Never give the seller more than 24 hours to accept your offer.
12. Use third-party stories when explaining why your logic is more valid than the seller's logic.
13. Casually remind the seller of the peace of mind and weight off the shoulders he/she can expect once the property is sold.
14. Stay calm. Don't blow your cool. If tension seems to be rising, change the subject.

15. Blame your inflexibility on someone or something else. Your lawyer or your accountant or your budget serve this purpose well.
16. Be a good listener; and once you make a telling point, quietly wait as long as necessary for the other person to speak.
17. Don't ever fall in love with a property. Love kills objectivity. When objectivity vanishes, so do negotiating skills.
18. Let the seller know you're looking at other properties as well as this one.
19. Re-read the "multiple offer" concept described in this chapter . . . and use it.
20. Use nonessential contingencies as a negotiating maneuver.
21. Where there is only a small amount of equity, use the net/net offer principle.
22. If negotiations seem to be stalled, leave the paperwork and give the seller the option to contact you before a certain time that same day.

Okay, got all those? Don't worry if you can't remember them all as you start out. They'll soon become second nature. But until they do, refer to this page with each deal you're attempting to put together.

I'd say, "Good luck," but it doesn't fit the circumstance. Luck is secondary to negotiating, and if you can set up win/win circumstances you'll have all the success you can handle.

CHAPTER TWELVE

Who's in Charge Here?

(Suggestion: "Loners" walk an isolated path. The statement, "I can do it myself," may be the right way to go, or it might be false economy. Independence is not just the goal of the entrepreneurial real estate investor; it is the lifeblood. But independence doesn't mean bypassing expertise that can help us. Ask yourself: Do you have the time to do everything, or might you make more money and have more fun working with professionals? Each circumstance has its own set of parameters. Judge those parameters with an open mind. Professionals can be a major help . . . if you remember two factors: 1) you're ultimately in charge because you have ultimate responsibility; and 2) you leave emotion out of your decisions.)

YOU'RE FREE-THINKING, INDEPENDENT, AND CAPABLE . . . BUT . . .

The whole idea of real estate investing, as we look at it in these pages — and as, I hope, you'll look at it when you apply the principles in these pages — is independence. You don't have to rely on others. You're your own boss. You have no master.

So is it a contradiction for me to suggest you lean on others, especially if they are specialists who can help you? Not at all. Their help makes your position easier, more practical, and more secure . . . which means your independence is more assured (and more quickly attained).

Do you remember that old television commercial, "Mother, please — I'd rather do it myself!"? The concept behind that commercial was that someone's independence was threatened. I say firmly: Your independence is *not* threatened when you call in professional help, any more than a doctor's independence is threatened when he/she asks for a second opinion from a specialist; or the President's independence is threatened when he appoints an ambassador or cabinet member or names a committee of experts to study a problem and recommend a solution.

I have had many conversations with self-made millionaires — captains of industry and commerce who hadn't inherited wealth but climbed the ladder of success themselves. Every one of them agreed: "I couldn't have done it alone. I needed and welcomed the help of others."

And these statements were sincere. They didn't parallel the kind of automatic listing of names one hears during the Academy Awards telecast when a winner thanks a group of people. They were recognitions by *winners* that winning is usually a team effort. One person manages the team, designates the starting lineup and makes substitutions as needed; but it's a team. A manager can't win a baseball game and a coach can't win a football game, without a team.

Most of the very successful people I know and admire offer three reasons why they may need the help of others, and I believe every one of these three reasons is valid:

1. Each day has 24 hours. No person can stretch that number of hours. With many irons in the fire, many

"deals" to juggle, the smart entrepreneur designates responsibilities for areas in which others can function efficiently.

2. Synergy works — that is, one plus one often equals three or more. A combined effort produces greater results than the sum of individual efforts. That's the *team* concept.

3. The true entrepreneur doesn't worry about not being an expert in every field. Computer experts handle programming; that's their specialty. Automobile mechanics get the "ping" out of an engine. That's their specialty. Entrepreneurs run the team. That's *our* specialty. Besides, your highest dollar-per-hour activity will be finding good deals.

THE VALUE OF ATTORNEYS

An old Danish proverb says, "Lawyers and painters can change white to black."

Imagine, though, structuring a complicated financial contract without a lawyer. Imagine instituting or defending a lawsuit without one.

Much of the disparagement heaped on lawyers is the result of the actions of a handful of practitioners. These are high-profile people, and the media expand reports of misdeeds to an extent and coverage beyond what they would do if it was an average businessperson.

But, on the other hand, as entrepreneurs, we need to understand that some lawyers feel they have to expand their role in a transaction. They want to comment not only on the legalities of the deal but on the business aspect underlying the deal as well. The statement, "Lawyers and accountants kill deals" stems from those who take this position.

So when looking for an attorney to handle some of your work, look for one who, like you, tries to find ways to *make the deal work* rather than ways to justify delaying or killing the deal.

Avoiding lawyers altogether can be an expensive mistake. The simple rule can be: When you don't feel comfortable with a pending contract or agreement or closing, that's when you call on an attorney.

Please don't wait until an hour before closing to start interviewing lawyers. Make your choice without heat. Even if considerable time passes between situations calling for legal help, stay in touch, on a casual or occasional lunch basis, with your lawyer. The friendlier and more open the relationship, the better it is for you.

And don't wait. Don't agonize over whether you need a lawyer or not. If you're agonizing over it, chances are you do need a lawyer. A good way to find one that is suited to your needs is to ask other investors who they use . . . then interview the candidates.

What will an attorney do? First, an attorney with a background in real estate can review your contract, telling you whether it is inadequate in any way. An attorney can prepare documents. An attorney may have connections for title insurance or provide that insurance. An attorney can physically handle the closing.

The right attorney probably won't charge you much more than a title company will charge, and you have the extra benefit of additional expertise. Ask up front how much the various services will cost and you won't face a nasty surprise.

One circumstance in which you positively should have a lawyer at your elbow: If you ever are sued or, for that matter, threatened with suit. And this very well may be a different lawyer from the one who handles your real estate transactions. (Your real estate attorney may be a good source for recommending a litigation attorney.)

Litigation runs in two directions. You may decide to file suit against a tenant or a contractor. The mere appearance of a letter from an attorney often resolves the matter. Again, ask what the services cost. A lawyer who regards himself/herself as "your" lawyer may write such a letter for little or no charge.

DEVELOPING RELATIONSHIPS

The smart real estate investor develops a first-name relationship with at least one banker and preferably two or three.

Oh, yes, you can buy property with no money down. You can buy property with bad credit or no credit. You can buy property when you have no cash. But if you want to become truly wealthy, with a net worth of several million dollars and a monthly cash flow of $30,000, you're going to have to have a banker on your side. At some point, you'll need a sizable line of credit to achieve these numbers.

Simple psychology is at work here. Get to know your banker. When you're in the bank, stop at your bank officer's desk for a moment and ask for an opinion *not* related to your own business. You'll establish that magical relationship, *rapport*. Don't worry about not bringing up your own business deals or prospective deals. That will come later.

Once again the subject of real estate brokers comes up. A broker who belongs to the National Association of Realtors may call him or herself a Realtor. Here, the discussion will be brief: A Realtor who has access to the multiple listing service and has had experience in rental properties is pure gold for you.

(Several of my "students" tell me they have solidified the relationship with a local broker by sharing the concepts covered in this book. Consider a thank-you, birthday, or

> Today I made offers on two different homes. One is an REO priced at $42,500.00 with a value of $59,000.00. My offer was for $34,230.00 cash. The other home is priced at $59,000.00, valued at $62,000.00, and I made an offer of $39,640.00 cash. This will make a great rental that will bring in about $600 a month.
>
> I recently purchased a nice 3-bedroom home priced at $52,000. After fixing it up, I was able to refinance it and pocketed $53,800!
>
> One reason I am able to put so many offers on the table is that I have found a great Realtor who really knows what kind of deals to look for and is not at all reluctant to present any offers for me. She really has worked for her commissions in the past two months.
>
> With her help and that of others who have begun to make referrals to me, my success seems to be getting better and better. In the past year, I have pocketed over $110,000, just by buying real estate.
>
> — *Bill H. Hayes, North Carolina*

holiday gift to a broker with whom you're in the process of establishing a rapport: A gift-copy of this book.)

Brokers can be an extra set of eyes and ears. "For sale by owner"? That's for *you;* direct. A broker's listing? That's where your own friendly broker can enter the arena.

You may encounter a broker who has the same working philosophy you do, who also invests in property. So what?

You may encounter other real estate investors, some of whom actually compete with you. So what?

There are more properties in your local marketplace, owned by sellers whose wants and needs change daily, than a thousand investors could ever purchase. Don't worry about competition. In fact, learn from others who either are in our business or are suppliers to our business.

If a real estate investment club exists in your area, join that club. Here's why: You'll find that it is not only educational, but motivational as well, to be around others who are trying to accomplish the same goals you are working towards. And, a great deal of property is bought and sold among members of these clubs.

POTENTIAL PARTNERS EXIST. FIND THEM.

People will want to become involved as your partner in buying a property. The only caveat: Don't accept a partner when you have a "gut feeling" this person is going to be a worry-wart or a troublemaker — in other words, one whose investing goals are not congruent with yours.

Explore the opportunity to take in partners. You may not need a partner for one of your purchases but good business judgment suggests you allow a partner to occasionally join you. That person (or group, and the cash they bring to the table), becomes an asset when you decide to make an offer on a major piece of real estate you simply can't handle alone.

Don't worry about partners edging you out. You're the expert.

APPRAISERS AND ACCOUNTANTS

Most banks have a list of "approved" appraisers. But the question in your mind has to be: Do I really need an appraiser?

You need an appraiser when a bank or other lending institution insists on a professional appraisal. That's obvious enough. What isn't so obvious *(and what I'm about to tell you is so powerful)* is your capability of leading the appraiser to the figure you propose to offer (which naturally has to be realistic). You meet with the appraiser to discuss the assignment. You say to the appraiser, "You might save some time by taking a look at my analysis of this property. I've concluded that it's worth about $150,000. I'd appreciate it if you'd call me before you start the job if you think you'll have a hard time coming in somewhere near that figure."

The operative phrase here is "before you start the job."

Work with appraisers as you do with lawyers and accountants and bankers. Try to establish rapport. Rapport will pay off big in both candor and cooperation.

I've had appraisers say to me, "Thanks for your analysis. It will save me some time." I've had appraisers say to me, "Thanks for telling me the figure you're looking for." I've also had the feeling, *many times,* that other appraisers would have said something similar but felt saying anything would be unprofessional.

When a lending institution requires an appraisal, ask for their list of approved appraisers. Also, ask whether they require a "full narrative" appraisal or whether a "short form" appraisal will suffice. Then call each appraiser and ask for a quote. As part of your discussion, you might ask, informally, "Offhand, would it be helpful if we met before you start the job, so I can share my feelings about value with you?" You'll not only get a feel for the type of person the appraiser is, but you'll begin establishing a relationship as well.

Accountants are another group of professionals who can save you taxes (and headaches).

The only type of relationship to have with an accountant is one in which you can pick up the phone and call with a question. Your accountant, once established as your ally, may well know as much about your affairs as you do. You want to be able to draw on advice that, applied, will minimize the tax consequences. Unless you yourself are an accountant, once you own several properties you should take the businesslike step of having an accountant take responsibility . . . not for day-to-day bookkeeping but for backup, recommendations, and preparation of tax returns.

TITLE COMPANIES, MANAGEMENT COMPANIES, AND RENTAL COMPANIES

A title company performs some of the same functions as an attorney in handling closings, except they don't render legal advice. Experience (and asking questions) will tell you whether a lawyer or a title company will be a better choice for a particular property you are purchasing.

The purpose of involving a title company is to be sure the title to the property has no defects; to prepare the paperwork; to verify any mortgage balances or other outstanding obligations; to provide title insurance (which will pay you if there is a problem with the title); to provide a trust account for depositing monies from the buyer or seller; to physically handle the closing; and to disburse funds, as requested.

An absolute rule: Never try to handle the closing yourself and never buy a property without obtaining title insurance.

One consideration is convenience. A title company (or lawyer) whose offices are geographically proximate to yours will be a time-saver for you.

A management company is another specialist available to help you. The typical fee they charge for managing a small rental property you own is 10 percent (but it's negotiable). As you enter the world of real estate investing, initially manage your own properties. You'll get an education that will be invaluable when, ultimately, you hire a management company for one or more of your properties. But when *you* do, there's no question about who's in charge: You are. The benefit is one of time-allocation. When you reach the point at which you realize you honestly understand the management business and that you can make more money buying properties than managing them, it's time to call in a management company. This is especially true for multi-family units or business properties.

Management companies are expected to know what rent rates should be and what typical vacancy rates can be expected. Management companies can assist you in another profitable way. Often a management company will know what properties are on the market or (better yet) about to come on the market. The company also will know which parts of town you might be better off avoiding.

A property rental company differs from a management company in that the sole function of a property rental company is to find tenants. Some are structured to get paid by the tenant, who is looking for an apartment or house; others are paid by the landlord when they locate an acceptable tenant.

Should you establish a relationship with a property rental company? As is true of so many professional relationships: It can't hurt, and they can be a valuable source of information even if you don't use their services.

ALLIES OR ADVERSARIES?

You may not have thought of some of these. Most are worthy allies; some can be deadly adversaries. Cultivating a relationship with all of them can be very much to your benefit.

You may need a pest control company to get rid of rodents and termites. Termites aren't as major a problem north of the Mason-Dixon line as they are south of it, but these destructive insects can destroy a house. If any question exists, ask a pest control company to inspect the house; if they find termites you probably can get the existing owner to agree to pay for their eradication.

City and county inspectors, on the other hand, can indeed be deadly adversaries as well as allies. While they are bound by various codes and regulations; they have the power to interpret them. Too, they can extend the amount of time allowed for compliance.

You certainly would understand the latitude available to them if you compare them with state police. Do you get a speeding ticket? Or do you get a "pass" or a warning? The option lies with them, and exercising the option one way or the other can be as dependent on what they think of you as it does on what they think of the violation.

Insurance agents now are far more valuable as allies than they were even a few years ago. The seemingly increased number of hurricanes, tornadoes, earthquakes, and floods has spawned a terrifying round of increases in insurance rates. In years past, our best bet was an agent who was a direct employee of one insurance company. That seems to have changed, at least in some areas. Insurance brokers, representing several companies, might be able to get you better rates, better coverage, or both. The obvious recommendation: Get competitive quotes.

EVERY CONTACT IS A GOOD CONTACT

When you own property, a plethora of suppliers, tradespeople, public officials, and technicians can make your life easier or more miserable.

Landscapers and tree-trimmers can not only beautify your property but come to your aid when a problem hits. For example, when Hurricane Andrew slashed through Florida a few years ago, two days later I hurried to visit a friend whose home lay directly in the storm's path.

After driving through blocks and blocks of reminders of the storm — branches everywhere, some trees totally uprooted — I was surprised to see his yard clean and unlittered. Some of the trees showed evidence of branches having been ripped away, but the branches themselves weren't on the ground. My friend explained that he had called the company that had handled his tree trimming for some years. They came to his house first and actually saved a palm tree that had been blown over, roots and all. (His neighbor had to wait six days for attention; by that time his tree was beyond saving.)

Some properties look "naked" because they have no landscaping. Adding some plants and trees work miracles and make the house look far more valuable than it did before. A landscaper can accomplish much on a minimum budget, whether to handle the plantings or just make recommendations, if you've established rapport.

Then we have surveyors. Whenever a bank is involved in the acquisition of real estate, a survey is required. (A survey is a good idea anyway, because it verifies the exact boundaries of the property.)

Surveyors not only may exhibit some flexibility regarding their fees; conversations with them can be quite profitable. They often have advance information regarding other parcels that either are or might soon become available.

Private building inspectors run the gamut from exceptionally useful to useless. In some states building inspectors have to be licensed; in others, not. But licensed or not, these are people we hire to be sure the foundation isn't settling, the air conditioner isn't about to conk out, the roof will remain leak-proof for another few years, the basement won't leak, and the wood trim isn't infested with carpenter ants.

Lenders usually require the use of an inspector only for bigger properties — usually, multi-family dwellings. For single family homes, a logical approach is for the buyer to look over each element carefully. If something seems to be awry — tiles cracked in one direction, a sagging roof, water stains on ceilings or the tops of walls, spongy siding — then bring in a building inspector.

And to conclude:

Your most valuable alliance might be with a "bird dog." This is anyone — *anyone* — who gives you a tip that results in a transaction. Reward bird dogs with cash and they'll become not only permanent members of your team but aggressive members of your team as well. A hundred or two hundred dollars for a successful referral of property (one that you actually purchase) can be very motivating. (A tip for a tip.)

In short: The more people with whom you have rapport, the easier your own life will be, the more you can accomplish, and the more money you'll save. Using other people's help can be as valuable as using other people's money. Together, those two elements are the perfect synergy: $2 + 2 = 5$.

CHAPTER THIRTEEN

Stoking Up the Profit Machine

*(Suggestion: One of the nastiest words in the world of real estate is **risk.** The professional real estate investor (that's you) dedicates himself or herself to minimizing risk. A couple of obvious ways to minimize risk are making the right kind of offer, being certain the written agreement matches the oral agreement, and exercising extreme care in the selection and examination of properties and timing of the offer. Add to these the frosting on the cake: Not having to "front" a considerable amount of money. Simple enough? Yes, if you don't let your heart overpower your head and if you have at your fingertips some of the risk-reducers outlined in this chapter.)*

SIMPLIFYING THE CONTRACT

Do you need a lawyer? Sometimes.

Some parcels have complicated legal titles. Some deals involve a whole bunch of small terms and conditions that have to fit together cohesively. And sometimes you'll encounter a seller who has *his* lawyer draw up a contract. When that happens, it's a good idea for you to have your own lawyer in the wings, because one thing is for certain: Another guy's contract, especially one drawn up by a lawyer, isn't going to throw benefits to you.

Understand, going in: No one is expected to be a legal expert *except* lawyers. So don't depend on anyone but a lawyer for legal advice. But the question in your mind might be: Do I need legal advice?

When you make an offer, that offer is not binding until the other party accepts it. Before that, it can be withdrawn at any time. Further, for a real estate contract to be enforceable, it must be in writing. Once the other party does accept it, though, it becomes legally binding on both of you. So be certain that (a) you mean what you say in an offer and are ready to perform under its terms, and (b) you impose a time limit for acceptance so that weeks and months from now you won't get a sudden acceptance of a long-forgotten offer, and (c) perhaps most importantly, you leave yourself an "out-clause" (sometimes referred to as a "weasel clause" or "escape clause"), such as "contract subject to Buyer's satisfactory physical inspection."

Stationery stores are full of pre-printed contracts. Half a dozen computer programs include real estate contracts in which all you have to do is fill in the names, addresses, and number of dollars.

Be careful of these, though, because almost all of them are tailored to benefit the seller. That's natural, because it's more likely that someone about to sell his home will want to have a pre-printed contract on hand than someone who just is fishing around, looking for property.

If a so-called boiler-plate contract (the standard wording in all contracts is called "boiler-plate") will suffice except for a handful of exceptions and/or additions, go ahead and use it. Be sure both parties initial any changes you've made in the preprinted sections, and attach as an "Adden-dum" — neatly typed, if possible — the exceptions and additions. In addition to initialing each change, both parties also should initial each page.

Understand, though, that these "boiler-plate" contracts are generally written to protect the seller. The contract that I provide with my course is absolutely written to protect the buyer. From the amount of money you have at risk, to the default period of a mortgage; from the responsibility the seller has for repairs, to the substitution of collateral clause, my contract is uniquely buyer-oriented. While in my home study course I have a definitive explanation of each element in a typical contract, just know that if you use my contract you are well-protected.

THE YELLOW BRICK ROAD: DISTRESSED PROPERTIES AND FORECLOSURES

Here's a truism for you: One of the fastest ways to make money in real estate investing is to buy distresed properties substantially below their market value.

The operative term: *Distressed properties.*

Two major types of distressed properties are available to real estate investors: Foreclosures and run-down properties. Read the next few pages carefully, because distressed properties can literally make you rich . . . if you know what you're doing.

Some distressed properties aren't really "distressed" at all. It's their owners who are distressed. This could be because of a money shortage but it also could be because of death, divorce, losing a job, or moving to another town.

A really distressed property may have broken windows, sagging fences, overgrown yards, peeling paint, and an overall rundown appearance. Don't let that stop you. Take the condition into account as you make an offer. You know this property isn't going to be brimming with bids, because the owner knows full well that "as is" isn't as attractive as "as it might be." Aha! You know this too.

Many so-called distressed properties, however, are not in as bad a condition as just described. Many properties, with some paint, some minimal landscaping, and a sweep with a lawn mower can take on an entirely new appearance and give a totally different impression. Many an investor will invest a few weekends in fixing and brightening and, as a result, claim far more than what was paid for the formerly-distressed property, either in equity or cash profits.

Don't recoil in disgust when you see such a property, unless the entire neighborhood looks that way. Oh, yes, you can make money in a bad neighborhood, but you also can face some problems no civilized person should have to face. You're better off looking for the worst house in the best neighborhood.

FORCED SALES AND FORECLOSURES

A homeowner goes bankrupt. Sometimes the bankruptcy laws let the owner keep the house and sometimes the bankruptcy court orders a sale. That's a forced sale.

A homeowner owes money for income taxes. The Internal Revenue Service orders a sale. Defaulted F.H.A., V.A., H.U.D., and conventional bank loans result in a forced sale. Houses seized as part of a drug arrest, some contested estates — a great many reasons can account for a forced sale.

Forced sales and physically distressed properties often go together. After all, someone who can't make the mortgage payment is unlikely to maintain the property. An abandoned house or one that has sat empty for a year isn't likely to be in tip-top shape. In fact, the longer a house sits vacant the more likely it becomes that vagrants will use it as a "crash-pad."

Even more, some owners, forced out, seem to take pleasure in leaving the biggest mess possible. You may see not only huge empty spaces where appliances are supposed to be, but a hole where the toilet is supposed to be. Instead of light fixtures, naked wires stick out of the walls and ceiling.

Should you acquire such property? Yes, but only if the price is right and you have the capability of putting it back into respectable condition.

Foreclosures are more and more common. One reason is the superabundance of credit cards and the ease of getting them. (After all, that's one area in which you now are an expert.) But a more telling reason is the gradual change in society's attitude toward bankruptcy. Our fathers and grandfathers would fight like tigers to avoid bankruptcy because such a move imprinted a permanent stigma on their lives. No more.

Also, some owners just walk away from a property. They decide they can't afford the payments; or they have so little equity they feel abandoning the property will cost them little; or they become hopelessly delinquent in their taxes. This is especially prevalent in big cities with declining neighborhoods.

The last decade of the twentieth century introduced a new element which is resulting in unexpected foreclosures — the adjustable rate mortgage.

Some of these "A.R.M.s" offered an artificially low starting interest rate. Once the initial period ended, rates began to climb. The homeowner, who was comfortable with the original terms, began to face higher and higher payments, sometimes totaling several hundred dollars per month *more* than the original terms. Result 1: Inability to pay. Result 2: Foreclosure.

Does this suggest that lending institutions like to foreclose?

Far from it. Banks lose money on foreclosures. Often they borrow money from the Federal Reserve in order to loan it out at a higher interest rate. That spread is how banks make money.

Now here comes a homeowner who has a 10 percent equity in his home and is three months in arrears in his house payments. He tells the bank, "I can't pay" . . . or disappears altogether. Now what? The bank not only has to go through the expensive legal procedure of foreclosure, but then has to put the house back on the market. What if that house remains unsold for six months or a year?

No, banks don't like foreclosures. But real estate investors do, because foreclosures can be quick bargain buys. (Notice, please: I didn't say "will be"; I said "can be.")

THE MECHANICS OF MORTGAGES

A mortgage is, to oversimplify, an acknowledgment that one party owes money to another and has pledged their property (in this case real estate) as collateral for repayment of that debt. If they don't pay, the one loaning the money can take the property. All mortgages are accompanied by a promissory note.

Usually, collateral for a mortgage loan is the house itself. The real estate becomes the security pledged to repay the loan. If the loan isn't repaid, the lender sues to get back the money. In the case of a mortgage, that suit is a foreclosure.

Here is where a complication can set in, and this is a reason banks tend to foreclose only when they feel the mortgage loan is a lost cause: A mortgage is a *lien* (the right to take and sell as security for a debt) on the property. The homeowner can have as many mortgages as he is able to obtain. We all know the term "second mortgage." It's common enough.

(When the famous Fontainebleau Hotel in Miami Beach went through a foreclosure some years ago, it had 13 separate mortgages!)

What determines whether a mortgage is a first or second mortgage, or for that matter the thirteenth? Easy enough: The date when the mortgage is filed in the public records. In other words, the very first mortgage recorded is a "first mortgage," the next mortgage recorded is a "second mortgage" and so on. For a lender, a first mortgage is the safest because being in first position as a creditor means that if the property is ever sold, chances of being repaid all the money loaned are excellent.

As a point of law, when a lender forecloses, all mortgages *junior* to (more recent than) the one being foreclosed are eliminated (and paid off if there is sufficient money from the sale) . . . as is, obviously, the mortgage being foreclosed. So if a bank forecloses on the first mortgage and another bank or a private individual holds a second mortgage, that second mortgage could become worthless if the property doesn't sell for enough to have extra money after satisfying the first mortgage. This is why lenders are cautious when advancing money for a second mortgage: They want to be certain the first mortgage is current and that there is ample equity.

In my home study course, I trace the steps involved in a foreclosure and the opportunities that occur at each step. For our purposes in this book, one caveat: Be sure to get a title report before you buy any property. Typically, such a report will cost $50 to $100, and it can protect you against

> *A simple truism: The greater the amount of equity one has in a property, the easier it is to borrow additional monies, because the probability of the lender recovering the full amount of the loan if foreclosure occurs is greater.*

a headache that otherwise might result in a monetary loss. The report will tell you what liens and judgments exist, such as one by a credit card issuer or a hospital.

Sometimes a connection with a real estate broker or a daily scan of the real estate ads in the newspaper can be valuable when locating a property that hasn't yet been foreclosed, but is likely to be. A homeowner may be delinquent on the monthly payments and unable to make them. The lending institution may already have sent some warning letters. That homeowner doesn't want a foreclosure to be a permanent blemish on his credit record, so he asks a real estate agent if it's possible to effect a quick sale; or he runs a "Must sell quickly" ad.

Suppose that owner does have some equity in the home. He knows he's not only about to lose some or all of that equity; he's about to lose his credit standing.

You might say, once you've established basic rapport:

"Look, Jim, you owe about $2,000 in back mortgage payments. What I can do — and I can do it right now — is take over that $2,000 so it's off your back. I'll give you $500 to pay your moving costs. You give me the deed and it's a done deal. That way you're off the hook without having a judgment on your record."

If he says yes, everybody wins.

Before actually buying the property, check the title, be sure the mortgage is assumable, and look over the property to be sure no major physical problems exist.

Carleton, I must have seen your course 20 or 30 times before I actually bought it. At that time, I was a used car salesman, who had just gotten divorced. Soon after I bought your course, I was fired from my job. I never had any experience in real estate, but I was determined to get out of the situation I was in.

It's been one year since I bought your course, and I am now the proud owner of 7 properties, with a positive cash flow of about $2,000 a month. My first purchase, I netted $6,000 profit in one week! I even got cash back at closing on two of my properties, totalling $53,046. Thank you for everything, Carleton!

— *Bill Huey, Alabama*

MAKING BIG PROFITS FROM FORECLOSURES

As you can see, you needn't wait until a foreclosure is announced in order to negotiate. Obviously, if you are to make an offer in the pre-foreclosure period, you need sources of information.

Before a formal foreclosure proceeding has begun, you are always better off contacting the owner/borrower rather than the creditor. Sometimes the house will be vacant: The owner will no longer be living in the house . . . or may never have lived in it. Public records though should give you the owners address. Or, you might leave a note in the doorway or through the mail-slot with your phone number on it. The note should explain that you might be able to help the owner preserve his/her credit and even get some cash.

How could the owner receive cash, and how would this benefit you? This is where your creativity comes into play. Think for a moment to see whether you might come up with the solution, before reading on.

Any ideas? Here's mine:

Make an offer to the owner that you will bring the mortgage payments current. Offer to split any cash profit after you "rehab" the property and sell it or, if you're going to keep the property as a rental, give the seller a note and mortgage for his or her equity, which could be discounted and sold for cash.

---

*Try to negotiate for a foreclosed property **before** a foreclosure auction. Bidding at an auction is seldom the most profitable approach because you're competing against professionals who will bid against you. The lender will probably bid $1.00 over what the homeowner owes to gain title to it. The lender then may be more flexible at re-selling the property — possibly at a lower price than the auction will bring.*

When you negotiate with a bank to acquire a repossessed property, don't be awed by the circumstance. Bankers put on their shoes one shoe at a time, just as you do. Their first price and offer of terms is the same as any commercial negotiator's: Not necessarily the final price and terms.

Bank loan officers usually are quite willing to share their list of foreclosed properties. What harm can come of asking, "In your opinion, might you be flexible on any of these?" Or, "What'll it take to get this one off your books?" ("Off your books" will strike home to a banker.) If the bank officer says, "We're asking $90,000," that phrasing is your indicator: It's an *asking* price, not a *final* price.

In addition to bank foreclosures, federal and local government agencies have large numbers of properties they have seized for non-payment and later sold at genuine bargain prices. Three of these agencies are:

1. G.S.A. (General Services Administration) — handles the sale of government surplus properties, plus real estate connected with illegal activities such as drugs or arms smuggling.
2. I.R.S. (Internal Revenue Service) — sells foreclosures to the public for nonpayment of taxes.
3. County tax sales — sells property to redeem "tax certificates" sold by the county to pay delinquent taxes. This isn't as complicated as one paragraph of text may make it seem.

Warning: When you buy properties at a public sale, you get them in "as is" condition. You can't write additions or protective clauses into the sale.

(Note: There are actually a total of 16 governmental and quasi-governmental agencies that offer foreclosure opportunities, that I discuss in my graduate course entitled, "Cashing In On Foreclosures and Distressed Properties: A Step-By-Step Formula.")

RUN-DOWN PROPERTIES CAN BE PROFITABLE.

Even after all these years I still don't know why any homeowner will allow a blemished appearance, given the negative impact it will have on the value of their home. A coat of paint on the exterior or the ceilings, a repaired fence or sidewalk, even mowing the lawn can add considerable value.

But that's the kind of property you should look for. I'm not talking about a rotting ruin or burned-out shell or, worst of all, a deteriorating neighborhood. You want property whose apparent value will increase based on cosmetic improvements you will make.

And you want property whose repairs you can handle yourself. Be careful about buying properties that would require a building permit. Building permits automatically mean building inspectors . . . and building inspectors automatically mean bringing the house up to code, which could involve expensive repairs or structural changes you didn't even consider.

An easy rule of thumb when buying a "fix-up" property: The results should be worth $5.00 for every dollar you spend, and the job should be one you and your helpers, if any, can complete within two to four weeks.

A few tips for exterior improvements: Some of the minor improvements that often seem to add $5.00 to the value for every dollar you spend are a new front door (the psychology is obvious — this is what a prospect inspects first) . . . new exterior lights . . . a neat-looking garage door . . . shutters . . . some flowers around the entrance . . . patched cracks in the driveway . . . shrubs trimmed way back . . . and grass seed.

A few tips for interior improvements: Some of the minor improvements that often seem to add $5.00 to the value for every dollar you spend are washed windows and repaired broken windows . . . new faucets and sinks . . . wallpaper . . . new bathroom vanities . . . new light fixtures . . . complete repainting . . . new carpet.

In order, the three most important rooms in any house are the kitchen, the bathrooms, and the master bedroom. Attention to these can add many thousands of dollars to the apparent value of a home. Placing a microwave on the kitchen counter may cost you $100, but the image it projects will be worth at least five times that amount. That same ratio covers window shades and blinds.

The operative word for the exterior: Neatness. The operative word for the interior: Cleanliness.

Can you handle these repairs and fix-ups yourself? Or do you know a handyman who can do them? If so, look for properties in need of this kind of improvement. Be sure, though, that it's the house that's run down and not the neighborhood.

Suppose you don't have cash or credit cards (although we've covered, early on, how to get credit cards). How might you pay for these improvements? You might take in a partner. You might borrow from a friend or relative. Or you might make a deal with a contractor or carpenter to handle repairs, offering a split of the profits when the property is resold.

Incidentally, students are often perfect workers for this kind of fix-up. You don't need a professional who charges a premium to paint a wall or mow a lawn.

Rule of thumb: Look for properties which, after being fixed up, can offer you at least a $10,000 profit. That $10,000 profit should come after the cost of acquiring and fixing up the property **and** all holding costs, including a brokerage commission upon sale.

A FINAL WORD ON STOKING UP THE PROFIT MACHINE

If you follow the principles espoused in this book, you won't make the mistakes so many would-be investors make. They *guess;* you *know!*

So you won't let your heart rule your head.

You'll regularly check sources of foreclosed and distressed properties.

You won't go to an auction and get caught up in the bidding, overpaying in order to have the momentary triumph of having outbid others.

You won't pass up a property because "it just doesn't look pretty."

You won't call in a crew of high-priced repair people and decorators to spiff up a property at an expense you won't get back in resale.

You'll have your profit machine running in high gear!

CHAPTER FOURTEEN

Managing Property While Still Maintaining Your Sanity

*(Suggestion: If all you think about is buying property, your attitude is similar to that of a person who takes a vacation and thinks only about getting there or getting home. It's what you do when you get there that makes the vacation complete. Think of real estate investing as you would think of any business enterprise. You buy a business. Then what? How do you run it? How do you make it more attractive to customers than it was before you bought it? What steps should you take to assure yourself that if and when you re-sell the business you'll make a profit? This same attitude should drive your thinking about real estate investing . . . because real estate investing not only **is** a business; it can be the most wildly successful business venture of your life.)*

MONEY: THE ASPIRIN FOR MANAGEMENT HEADACHES

There's no way to avoid the terminology.

If you own a house or an apartment and somebody else is living in it and paying you rent, you're the *landlord* and the other party is the *tenant*.

Somehow, in our society, the word "landlord" has achieved a nasty overtone. The image is one of a whip-cracking, humorless money-grubber, taking advantage of a decent, hardworking family that pays and pays and pays and then, the one month in which they can't pay the rent because the youngest child is ill with accompanying doctor bills, they're out in the snow.

Nawwwww.

Property management is one of the most misunderstood — maybe *the* most misunderstood — areas of real estate investing. And it isn't the most profitable area of real estate investing. So buying property will make more money for you than managing that same property.

Nonetheless, again my advice is: For the first few properties you buy, you should manage those properties yourself . . . for two reasons:

First, you'll save money. If another person or a management company manages the property, you pay a percentage of the rent. That money, at least when you're first starting out, should find a better home in *your* pocket.

Second — and this is far and away a more important reason — if you're seriously into real estate investing, you should learn the management business. You should know what problems beset the real estate manager. That way, when you reach the point at which you hire a manager, you'll know how to manage the manager.

STRUCTURING THE LEASE

Some tenants are friends. Some tenants are adversaries. You can't always predict in advance which will be which.

So the lease becomes the blueprint of the firm, definitive relationship between you and a tenant. If that blueprint is muddy, if some of the lines aren't drawn clearly, the potential for conflict exists.

Special circumstances attending any specific lease should be written into the lease. Remember Samuel Goldwyn's famous malaprop: "A verbal contract isn't worth the paper it's written on."

An important consideration should be that when the tenant has moved into the premises, the tenant acknowledges that everything is in good working order: The appliances and water heater work, the plumbing plumbs, the walls aren't defaced, the furnace and air conditioner are operable.

Consider having your tenant become responsible for maintaining the property. If you have a security deposit — and you should — this becomes at least a minor guarantee that the place won't be left in a shambles. (I'll discuss security deposits shortly.) At the very least, the lease should spell out that the tenant should cover a percentage of repair costs incurred while occupying the premises, particularly in a single-family home (it's more difficult to do this with multi-family properties). This avoids capricious demands for repairs and also assures better care of the property.

---

*A tip that can make money and save headaches: Build in an **incentive and penalty** system. Charge a higher rent than you originally intended, offering a discount for payment by the fifth of the month. You can advertise this feature. The word "discount" has a magical effect in an ad, as you undoubtedly already know.*

Tenant turnover costs money. Offering an additional incentive for a lease of 15 to 18 months may be a moneysaver, because that means three to six additional months in which the relationship with the existing tenant is a "given." Studies have shown that tenants who stay more than a year are likely to renew their leases.

If you're an adventurer, you can squeeze extra money out of a lease by asking for payments on a bi-weekly basis rather than on a monthly basis. Here's an example:

Suppose instead of charging $400 per month you ask for $200 every two weeks. The calendar works in your favor. A rent of $400 per month totals $4800 per year. But a year holds 52 weeks. That's 26 payments of $200 — $5200. You've added $400, an entire extra month, to the year's total. (Having absorbed that, absorb this as well: You have to collect rents slightly more often. Is it worth your time? Only you can answer that one.)

I have learned that managing property is a science, not a seat-of-the-pants batch of guesses. Thanks to your solid lists of procedures and checklists, I have been able to avoid some of the problems and pitfalls I hear others discussing. I feel that I am a good landlord. My tenants respect me and I am paid on time every month.

A little over a year ago, I was just coming out of a bankruptcy. Today, because of my investing, my net worth has gone to over $1 million and my positive cash flow is $120,000 every year.

— *Bruce Carlin, Utah*

If you have multiple properties or a multi-family dwelling, be sure all rents are due on the same day of the month, preferably the first. You may inherit circumstances in which the existing tenant moved into the place on the twelfth, so rents have been due on the twelfth. Don't continue the mistake the previous manager made. If the tenant is not on a lease, tell them that rents are now due on the first; so this month, all the tenant owes is 18 days' rent. If they are on a lease and won't cooperate, this process will have to wait until renewal time. If you want to be especially benevolent, offer a $10 rebate "because I know this is a little bit of trouble for you."

A security deposit is mandatory, both for your peace of mind and as responsible business practice, but it should always be more or less than the monthly rent. You don't want tenants to look upon their security deposit as rent payment. Typically, you'll ask a tenant for the first month's rent, the last month's rent, and a security deposit.

Many times, the prospective tenant will complain — or feel, even if the complaint isn't verbalized — that this is too much money to part with. Offer an option: You'll personally finance that last month's rent, to be paid over the next four months. The tenant pays only the first month and the security deposit right now. If payment for the last month's rent extends beyond four months, you'll have to charge 10 percent interest. That's a fair deal, and avoiding the 10 percent penalty usually impels the tenant to pay the last month's rent within that four month window.

Incidentally, I never refer to a tenant as a "tenant." It sounds cold, harsh, and demeaning. I will refer to them by name, or, if I'm sending a form letter or notice, I will refer to them as a resident (e.g., "Dear Resident").

Don't ever let a tenant move in until that individual has given you either cash, a certified check or a personal check that has had time to clear the bank. No exceptions, unless you like to play Russian Roulette.

THERE ARE GOOD TENANTS . . . AND BAD TENANTS.

You have the power to set the tone of your relationship with your tenant. A very good idea is to give tenants a house plant or a basket of cut flowers when they move in. Also, you can make a file of birthdays (the birth date usually appears on an application for residency). Send a birthday card. Send a holiday card. For particularly pleasant and cooperative tenants, a bottle of champagne on New Year's Eve is a gift that will be remembered, especially if you deliver it yourself.

When a tenant asks for a special service or dispensation you don't want to honor, instead of replying with a flat "No," your answer can be worded to shift responsibility for the eventual "No" to an outside source: "I'll have to check with my partner on that," or, "Gee, I wish I could, but my partner would skin me alive."

Will you ever face the ugly prospect of evicting a tenant? Yes, even if you use one of the national "tenant-qualification" services that exist around the country (and you should). Who knows? Sometimes a landlord/tenant relationship that has existed for a number of years will go sour. Rent payments cease. "Junker" automobiles appear on the lawn, in defiance of the lease. Neighbors complain about the noise or even the smell.

If you find yourself in a position in which you have to remove a tenant, I offer three options. As you absorb these options you may understand even better why screening tenants before they occupy your property is a sound idea.

The first option is the legal option. Every state has a formal eviction process. Usually the first step is a formal written notice to the tenant to vacate the property. That may be enough with some tenants. But if the tenant ignores the written notice to vacate, you then get a Writ of Eviction at the courthouse. If that doesn't move the tenant, you then go back to the courthouse and get a Writ of Possession. Now you're in total command, because if the tenant ignores the Writ of Possession you call in the sheriff. A deputy physically removes the tenant and any possessions (or watches you do it). Depending on the state (and your own state of mind) the entire process can take anywhere from two or three weeks to three months.

The second option is a group of illegal moves (which I personally don't agree with or condone). One is the "Sneaky Pete" option, where the landlord has to send the front door or even the toilet out for repair, or turn off the electricity and/or the water. If you have tremendous guts, you can try one of these, but you can get sued . . . or shot at. This really isn't a logical (or legal) option except for those who thrive on controversy (and lawlessness).

The third option is what I call the Carleton Sheets Eviction Procedure. I offer it to you here. Take my word for it, the first time you use it, the procedure will be worth many times the cost of this book.

I said earlier in this chapter that when the fifth day of the month passes and a tenant hasn't paid, the discount no longer applies and the full amount becomes due. Sometimes a tenant will pay a part of the rent, pointing out a misfortune that has occurred. Usually, the partial payment is accompanied by a promise that the rest will be paid in weekly installments over the rest of the month. Invariably, this is a prelude to disaster, because by the end of the month, when theoretically the last overdue payment has been made, another month's rent is due. Where is *that* money supposed to come from? If you as landlord are overly benevolent, you can — and probably will — wind up as the victim.

I tell the tenant I have another prospective tenant who is eager to move in *immediately.* In fact, they've sold the home they owned, or the building they lived in is being demolished, or they have just moved from another city. "They have to get in here right now. How soon can you move out?"

Invariably the tenant will plead or argue for an extension to the end of the month. Instead of joining the argument — a mistake, because you shift the relationship into an adversarial one — answer, "I'll tell you what." Those four words have a magical effect, because they suggest compromise even when compromise isn't intended.

"I'll tell you what: If you'll vacate now — well, in the next three days — I won't take this to the credit bureau, which could seriously damage your credit. And I won't bring suit against you in court for the balance of the unpaid rent, which would cost you a lot of money in legal fees."

The tenant may be unmoved: "My credit is shot anyway. Go ahead, take me to court. I have nothing to lose."

That's when the trump card comes into play: "Help me out, here. These people are ready to move in. I'll tell you what: I'll not only forget what you owe, I'll give you $300 if you're out of here in 24 hours."

Understand: You're sitting with a security deposit and the last month's rent. These become bargaining weapons. It's the tenant's money you're giving back. Don't hesitate doing that if the situation calls for it. You might extend the move-out period — grudgingly — to three days. But don't let a misguided sense of compassion cause you to let rents go unpaid. That's not only the short road to losing money, it fails to recognize that in a reverse situation your tenant wouldn't have the same compassion for you.

DEALING WITH A FEE-PAID RENTAL COMPANY

Not all property management companies are the same. In the past few years, a different type of company has appeared, especially in the major metropolitan areas. This is the "Fee-Paid Rental Company."

Fee-paid rental companies can be helpful allies for us real estate investors. Their purpose is to help people find apartments and rental homes. Usually the tenant pays nothing; the landlord pays a flat fee upon accepting the tenant.

Before you reject the notion of paying a fee to get a tenant, consider two points: First, where would you find a tenant? If you run an ad in the newspaper you're paying something to the newspaper, with no assurance that the ad will pull any applicants. This fee applies only if the fee-paid rental company finds you an acceptable tenant.

Second, note that phrase "acceptable tenant." The company may do some screening in advance. Typically, an undesirable tenant will not register with a fee-paid rental company but will look for a greedy or desperate landlord.

DEALING WITH A PROPERTY MANAGEMENT COMPANY

The Yellow Pages are not a reliable source for a property management company. But if you have no other options to explore — friends or real estate brokers or other real estate investors you can talk to regarding referrals — this may be the basis for choosing.

My suggestion parallels the suggestion I would make if a doctor told me I need brain surgery. I'd ask for another opinion. In the world of real estate management, this means interviewing two or three property management companies to get a "feel" for their philosophy and competence.

In choosing a property management company, seven separate elements should drive your choice. Ask these seven questions; then make your decision based on your composite determination of which company best answered the questions to your satisfaction.

1. What percent commission do you charge for finding tenants? (One-half of one month's rent is reasonably standard).

2. What percent of the gross rent do you charge for managing a rental property? (Percentages range from six percent to 10 percent. Don't be afraid to negotiate, because often this number is flexible and may even differ among the various type properties the company manages.)

3. Do you charge an "override" on repair or maintenance bills? That is, if you hire a carpenter or a plumber or an electrician, do you tack a fee on top of the actual charge? (Some property management companies do — as much as 10 percent, which can be a hefty chunk — and some don't. Some claim that they don't but arrange a "kickback" from service workers.)

4. If I decide to sell the property during the term of the management agreement, do you insist on the right to list it? (Don't allow this.)

5. Do you provide monthly or quarterly income/expense statements? Are these statements computerized? (A computerized statement tends to be more "valid" because more people may be involved in their preparation. But if a company wants to cheat you, it makes no difference if the statement is computerized or not. The principal advantage of a computerized statement is its completeness and arithmetical accuracy.)

6. Can you please tell me the names of three other persons or companies whose properties you're managing? (Assume that the property management company will give you the names of those with whom it has the best relationships. Check not only the references but the apparent condition of the buildings being managed.)

7. Will you agree to a mutually-enforceable 60-day cancellation clause? (A smart management company will have no objection to such a clause because these people know they will satisfy you. You want the clause in case they don't.)

A few general notes about these seven qualifiers:

If you use the "tight" lease I've recommended, this should be a solid reason for the management company giving you the most favorable terms. The tenant has agreed to assume at least partial responsibility for maintenance and repairs, and that agreement means less work for the management company. Invariably, when a tenant is spending his own money, capricious expenditures disappear.

If the management company says, "We'll charge you 4 to 8 percent for finding a tenant, 10 percent of the gross income as a paid management fee for single-family homes, and a 6 to 7 percent management fee for multi-family dwellings," that's in the ball park.

Insist on an agreement not exceeding one year; an agreement that does not automatically give the management company the right to list the property if you decide to sell it within the year; and an agreement that includes the 60-day mutual cancellation clause.

Don't be intimidated when the agent for a property management company flashes a form and says, "See right here? It's standard."

Nonsense. Whoever put a clause or a paragraph into a contract can take it out.

These agreements are prepared by the property management company to favor the property management company, as if to say "See right here? It's printed into the contract. We didn't single *you* out for this. It's standard." More nonsense.

"Standard" is a point of departure, not a law. Some real estate beginners are afraid to attack a pre-printed contract, especially one that says "Standard" at the top. Go ahead and write "chicken-scratch" all over it. If the changes are initialed by both parties, then "standard" has the definition it should have — agreed to by both and favoring neither.

GOVERNMENT SECTION 8 PROGRAM

Section 8 of the Housing and Community Development Act of 1974, was created to assist low income people in finding "safe, decent and sanitary housing". The program is administered by local Public Housing Agencies (PHA's), frequently called Housing Authorities. With over 3,000 of these across the country, chances are good that you'll find one in your city or county.

It's the responsibility of the PHA to evaluate applicants for assistance, inspect properties that have been put into the program and finally, to make rental assistance payments to owners.

To place your property into the program, merely find a Section 8 approved tenant (you might advertise: "Section 8 OK"), check on the tenant's suitability as you would with any other non-Section 8 tenant (forget about a credit check, however. Their credit will undoubtedly be a disaster), notify the local PHA that you wish to have your property inspected and, assuming it passes, the tenant will move in. From that point on, you will receive two payments; One from the tenant and one from Uncle Sam. I say two, and yet with at least one of my properties, the PHA pays the entire rent amount.

To learn more, see my course, "The Painless Guide To Property Management," (available through the Professional Education Institute) or contact your local Housing

Authority office (easily found in the white or green pages of your telephone directory).

15 TIPS FOR HASSLE-FREE PROPERTY MANAGEMENT

Here is a handy checklist of fifteen tips to consider when you own and manage rental property. You may not want to observe them all; after all, just as every property is different, every tenant relationship also is different.

The purpose of these tips is to give you ammunition so you won't inadvertently wind up in an embarrassing position, in a state of negative cash flow, or in an unwanted adversarial relationship with an undesirable tenant.

Tip 1: Never let a tenant move into a property until the entire amount agreed upon has been paid, either in cash or with a certified check; or until a personal check has cleared. This may be the standard first month, last month, and security deposit; or you may agree to more lenient terms. But enough property managers have a drawer full of personal checks upon which the bank has stamped "Insufficient funds" to make all of us cautious about allowing a move-in until a personal check has been fully credited to your account.

Tip 2: Ask the tenant to complete a "Move in/Move out Form" when first occupying the premises. Items in need of repair or replacement should be listed.

Tip 3: Inform tenants *in writing* that your insurance doesn't cover their own personal property. Encourage them to obtain tenant insurance. It's inexpensive and protects them against damage they or one of their guests might inflict on the property or damages from a fire that occurs. If you don't give them this notice in writing, the area of responsibility remains muddy and might be the nucleus of a messy disagreement or lawsuit if damage does occur.

Tip 4: Tell all tenants that rents are due on the first of the month. If you want to offer an apparent discount for early payment by the fifth, that is fine, but rents are due on the first. Implementing this policy will ease your management job immeasurably.

Tip 5: If no drapes or curtains are in the residence, don't provide them. If drapes and curtains are in place and they become soiled or threadbare, don't replace them. Yes, we all know that adding curtains and drapes can make a big difference in the appearance and desirability of a desolate-looking residence, but once provided, that's it. Your responsibility is finished. And if you attract a tenant to a house or apartment that has no drapes, that's exactly the way you intend it. If the tenant wants drapes, fine — it's up to him/her to get them. (But please, no sheets over the windows.)

Tip 6: Set the monthly rent $25 to $50 higher than the amount you must have; then offer an incentive discount of the same amount for prompt payment. (See Tip 4, above.)

Tip 7: Never show a vacant rental property to a prospective tenant unless it is ready for occupancy. People are easily "turned off" by another's mess and filth.

Tip 8: If you've been looking for a tenant for more than two weeks and have had no action or someone who says, "I'll think it over," with no subsequent contact, consider adding a rental incentive such as a microwave oven or a color television set. These have an incentive-value well beyond their cost and not only can save you further advertising costs but also can result in earlier rental income. Remember, an annual lease could well be a $5,000 to $10,000 contract.

Tip 9: The appliances are yours. They belong to you. Tell tenants you are willing to loan the appliances for the duration of the lease but you are not responsible for maintaining or repairing them. If anything happens to the appliances, the tenants have an option: Repair them or replace them. If a tenant wants a dishwasher or a garbage disposal, that's up to the tenant. These are optional appliances, and unless they are there when you acquire the property (or unless you decide to live in the residence yourself) there's no reason to provide these items. Count on appliances being abused. When a tenant has access to something he/she doesn't own, care and maintenance aren't always in mind. Sometimes, ovens are left on, bones are put into the garbage disposal, refrigerators are overloaded, stove burners are not cleaned . . . It just happens.

Tip 10: The security deposit should *not* be the same as a month's rent. That way, the tenant can never make a "But I thought I could use it for my final rent payment . . ." claim.

Tip 11: Consider offering a longer lease — say, 14 or 15 months. To make it more palatable to the tenant, suggest a lower rate or at least the same rate for this extended period of time, in exchange for a longer lease. This can even be something you advertise in the newspaper: "Discounted rent for a long-term lease." The "discount" comes from the tenants knowing they will not have their rent raised after 12 months. And besides, tenants who stay longer do save you both trouble and money.

Tip 12: Keep good records of each individual unit. This includes a record of exactly what color paint is on the walls, because if you want to match that paint later on your chances of an exact match — if you don't have the color and code number noted — are close to zilch. Keep a record of your maintenance and repair costs for each unit. Also, keep instructions, owner's manuals, and warranties on furnaces, air conditioners, ovens, refrigerators and other appliances. And need I add — keep extra keys, tagged with proper identification, in a safe place.

Tip 13: Note my "Carleton Sheets Eviction Procedure" for the situation in which you have a problem tenant. Offer a monetary reward for quick vacating. And by quick I mean 24 hours, or at most three days. If you give them a week or more, they tend to settle back in and you have to start all over again.

Tip 14: Join your local apartment association or investors' club. You'll make valuable contacts with other investment property owners and assure yourself of being current with new procedures and legal decisions. You also will have more access to properties for sale. If you don't know how to contact your association, call the National Apartment Association in Alexandria, Virginia. For local investor clubs in your area, contact the Professional Education Institute.

Tip 15: Check out a Section 8 tenant just like you would any other tenant. Don't assume the Housing Authority office has done this. People are accepted into the Section 8 program based on need, not for their suitability as tenants.

A CONCLUDING THOUGHT ABOUT PROPERTY MANAGEMENT

You can't just declare yourself a property manager, or at least a competent one. You should study the field, make contacts, and avoid making decisions before you think through the circumstances.

Well, now you have a solid understanding of the basics. You may want to learn more tips, techniques, and strategies about sound property management as you move forward in your investment program. Heaven knows, in over 25 years of managing both small and large properties, I've seen just about every situation come up.

I'm proud to say that because I've enjoyed sound screening practices, coupled with respectful but firm behavior toward my tenants, I've had very few negative incidents. I have put together a course including a comprehensive manual and six audiotapes. It contains everything I know about property management, entitled "The Painless Guide To Profitable Property Management," and it's available by contacting the Professional Education Institute.

Managing property can be an extra profit center or it can be a curse. Which one it turns out to be is up to you and the way you establish your landlord/tenant relationships.

People who own one rental unit who tell you they have had good luck with their tenants are probably having just that — "Good Luck." You'll find though, as you acquire many units, that luck is not an ingredient in the management stew. Judgement is though, and that comes from knowledge and an application of what you've learned . . . in other words, experience. You now have all the ingredients for a good management stew. So, enjoy!

CHAPTER FIFTEEN

Other Important Aspects of Real Estate Investing

(Suggestion: From the very first day you start your exciting "second career" as a real estate investor, you will begin the process of building your base of negotiating knowledge. This book gives you the tools. Your own experiences will refine the use of those tools. Please regard the book as a working partner. Don't be afraid to underline or highlight passages . . . to make notes in the margins . . . to put in your own words, based on your own experiences, some of the useful occurrences that sharpen your own professionalism. This chapter covers bits and pieces not covered elsewhere. Most welcome would be a note from you to me, suggesting inclusions in future editions based on your own successes . . . or even temporary failures.)

HERE COMES THE TAX MAN

You know perfectly well why I haven't been more specific about the tax advantages and consequences of real estate investing: They change with the wind.

You may remember the "tax shelters" of the early 1980s. They were a taxpayer's dream: We could buy into a tax shelter, take all kinds of deductions, and make money as the tax shelter lost money.

Blam!

Suddenly Congress changed all the rules, disallowed what they had promoted before, and left many investors with huge *unexpected* tax debt. So much for consistency.

If tax laws stayed the same, it wouldn't be necessary to publish all those paperback tax guides each year. But tax laws don't stay the same. That can be a blessing or a curse, depending on how they change, what the latest Internal Revenue Service interpretations are, and how you structure your transaction.

So before you go rushing off to form a corporate shell ... before you say to someone to whom you've sold a jointly owned property, "Make the check out to me personally" ... before you form a limited partnership with yourself as the general partner and all others as limited partners ... before you put all your properties in a trust ... you may want to bite the bullet and discuss the tax consequences with an accountant. But if you're not trying to get "fancy," taking title to property in your and your spouse's name would be a good start.

If you do go to an accountant, though, the time will be well-spent, but only if you have *specific* questions to ask and aren't just discussing theory. Theoretical answers are discouraging both to the person who asked the question and to the person answering the question. Neither is sure the answer has any relevance to an actual "battle conditions" circumstance.

A WONDERFUL TAX ALLY: DEPRECIATION

When you buy real estate, the tax laws (I'd better add: as of this writing) allow you to depreciate the value of the property — on paper, that is — at a rate that approximates about 3½ percent per year. So for each $1,000 you paid, you can take a deduction of approximately $35. That means after one year you've "devalued" the property, for tax purposes, to $965 per thousand. The second year, you again take a 3½ percent deduction, and on you go. This so-called paper expense didn't really cost you anything and yet you can deduct it from your gross income as if it did.

You can see the value of depreciation. It gives you a tax advantage. And you can also see how powerful this is, because we aren't describing property worth just $1,000. It could be $50,000 or $100,000, or, eventually, several million dollars.

The need for an accountant becomes more necessary when you sell the property and you're filing your tax returns, because if you've handled it right, you'll make a profit — not on the *depreciated* value but on the *actual* value, based on what you originally paid for it plus improvements, plus appreciation. You will have to pay tax on your profits: The selling price minus your depreciated cost, also known as basis. In the meantime, though, having that depreciation allowance is like getting an interest-free loan.

EXCHANGING PROPERTY

Once again we venture into strange waters, describing a moneymaker that results from the Internal Revenue Code. The Code allows you to exempt any profit from taxes if you *exchange* property with another property-owner rather than selling yours for cash. The key is: The property must be "like-kind."

Exchanges are a refinement you'll want to explore after you have some experience in real estate. After all, you can't think of an exchange until you have some property to exchange.

My home study course covers this intricacy. Or you can discuss the possibilities with an accountant or lawyer familiar with real estate tax laws.

"HI! I'M CARLETON SHEETS."

I used my own name because I don't know yours yet. If you decide to become a real estate investor, and have the good fortune so many others have had, a large part of the credit will have to go to your own *personal public relations.*

The days of the "Simon Legree" brutal negotiator and the days of the "Uriah Heep" whining negotiator both are, thankfully, on the wane. Today's successful real estate investor radiates three characteristics: Confidence, knowledge, and personality. That's an unbeatable combination.

When you greet somebody, announce your name with a friendly informality. "Hi!" is better than "How do you do." Friendliness is contagious.

"DIVE IN." AND THAT'S AN ORDER!

I have a friend who's an avid scuba diver. He tells me that when he and his group went out on the ocean to have their "certification dive" in 30 feet of water, they were loaded with information; they had tested every procedure in a deep pool; they had hooked up their equipment a dozen times. Still, about half the class couldn't attach their regulators to the tanks or did it wrong. Four people refused to go into the water at all. One fellow, who had taken the class with his young son, jumped into the water alongside his son, who promptly dived while the father hung onto the boat in a desperation hold. Fear overcame logic. "I made about ten dives before I had any confidence at all," my friend told me. "But the instructor made a mistake. He literally threw us into the water and told us to dive. A few words of encouragement might have kept that guy from his death-grip on the boat and turned him into a diver. As far as I know, he never did get certified."

Because of my real estate, I have a positive cash flow of three thousand dollars a month. My salary at the hospital where I work, is equal to what I bring in from the real estate and I could quit work today, if I wanted to.

I feel like women could do more, for themselves, and for their families and grandchildren, if they would just take that first step; just buy the course.

If their husband were to die or divorce or whatever, they would know they can make it. And it will make them feel so good to know that they did this on their own.

— *Arlene Crosby, Georgia*

Fear is the companion of inexperience.

Early on, many real estate investors give off an aura of fear so tangible you can almost smell it. Perhaps that shouldn't surprise me because I understand animals can smell fear. Still, some fear is normal. Let's face it, you're involved in a business negotiation with thousands of dollars on the table.

I have two pieces of advice, if you're afraid of actually going through with that first deal:

1. If you've done your homework and the numbers make sense . . . if you've checked the neighborhood and the property . . . if you're sure you've left your emotions out of the mixture . . . then plow ahead with confidence. You should be considerably more sure of the deal than most investors and even most brokers, who don't have your grasp of what to do and what not to do.

2. If after checking your numbers, inspecting the neighborhood and the property, and double-checking all the aspects you can think of, you're still uncertain . . . pass. Other deals will come up. Enthusiasm is a key component of success. And once you pass up a deal you later realize was gold-plated, you'll be more aggressive next time out.

DON'T TURN UP YOUR NOSE AT MOBILE HOMES

A generation ago, mobile homes were the stepchildren of real estate.

Most people didn't call them "mobile homes" then; the word was "trailers." The image was that of a beat-up trailer wobbling down a dusty highway behind a pick-up truck. When the truck reached its destination, the wheels came off the trailer, which then became permanent living quarters.

Today's mobile homes, though, are sometimes more lavish than conventional site-built structures. A national building code has resulted in stronger, more permanent mobile homes, and many have never seen the road at all.

In fact, we don't call them mobile homes any longer. Those produced under the code enacted in 1976 by the Department of Housing and Urban Development (H.U.D.) are *by law* called "manufactured homes." I use the term "mobile homes" here because most people have an easier time identifying what I'm talking or writing about.

For us as real estate investors, mobile homes — and the parks in which many of them are located — can be a real gold mine. Prices are low, competition is thin, and opportunities are often more abundant than is the case with conventional homes.

No question about it — the typical mobile home is priced well below the typical site-built home with the same square footage. Sometimes you can pick up five or six of them for what a house and lot three blocks away would cost.

You can make money buying a mobile home and renting it out. You may find that renting on this level is easy, and your risk is low because the number of dollars you're investing is low.

Or you might buy a mobile home that needs "rehabbing." Many of them do.

Or you can buy a lot in a mobile home park, put a new or rehabbed mobile home on it, and rent or sell it.

Because mobile homes are usually at the bottom end of the real estate scale, you can make quick money with an easy turnover to another investor. You'll buy one cheap and resell it for a fast $1,000 to $2,000 profit. Here's the opportunity:

Because mobile homes are at the bottom of the real estate scale, they seem to offer the only hope for real estate ownership by many people without money. When these folks buy a mobile home and then can't make the payments, you become a hero by offering to take over the payments and then give them a few hundred dollars to cover the cost of moving — as was discussed in an earlier chapter of this book. In some rare situations, I have even seen sellers come to the closing table with cash to pay the buyer to take their property.

When you buy a mobile home this way and resell to an investor, that's quick money; but it isn't where the real money is. The real money comes from reselling to an end-user. Careful, now! You may experience the same problems that allowed you to purchase the mobile home so inexpensively to begin with.

Occasionally an entire mobile home park is available for sale. Use the same discretion you'd use for a multiple-unit apartment building.

When considering a mobile home, inspect with unusual care the condition of the roof, the siding, the plumbing, and the electrical systems. The park itself is also a factor. Even the type of people living there is worthy of consideration.

A word of caution: Don't let an apparently low price or having to tie up only a few immediate dollars color your thinking. If you do that, emotion rules over intellect, and you're on your way to losing money.

You may think, "I'll put a thousand dollars in to spiff up this place, and that will add four or five thousand dollars to its value." If this were a site-built home, you'd probably be right. But rehabbing a mobile home doesn't pay off that way. Usually, if you put a thousand dollars in, you can expect to take an extra thousand dollars out. That isn't the way to get rich.

You can, though, and with less money, offer an incentive to swing an undecided buyer or tenant to take the property "as is." "Tell you what: I'll put in some new carpeting"; versus, "Tell you what: I want you to have this place. I'll pay the first month's mortgage [or lot rent], if you take the place now 'as is,'" can be a powerful motivator.

In my home study course, I have a great deal more to say about mobile homes and ways to make a lot of money from them, especially healthy cash flows. Right now, be satisfied to know that investment returns, at least on a percentage basis, can be astronomical if you approach mobile home buying and selling with the same dispassionate business sense you'd use for any other home. Lots of people are looking for a place they can afford. You can be their source.

CAPITALIZING ON PARTNERSHIPS

Throughout this text I mention the value of partnerships. Group investing is as old as the ownership of real estate itself.

What causes some potential partners to flee — or to look for holes in a deal — is the negative image so many "promoters" have cast as a shadow onto the concept of partnerships. You and I are the victims of that image generated by others who don't share our insistence on integrity.

> *Never go into a partnership with the idea of taking advantage of your partner or partners. Aside from being short-sighted, this attitude will result in your having an unsavory reputation you may never be able to shake. Honesty is not only the best policy; it's simply good business practice.*

The two most common ways to work with partners are either to have them loan you money or to have them become equity partners. (Often, if you want them as equity partners, originating the discussion on the basis of a loan will have them thinking, "Instead of making a few dollars on the loan, I wonder if I can get in on this.")

Don't solicit investors over the phone or by mail. If something goes wrong you can be in serious legal trouble. Who needs that?

Smart marketing might have you approaching potential partners *before* you have a specific purchase in mind: "I have real estate investments coming up all the time. Are you interested in being my partner if I find a good piece of property I think we can make money on? Oh, I'm not talking about big money. You can be in for $3,000 to $5,000."

And don't forget: The best referral for a new partner can come from an existing partner. That's especially true if you come upon a major possibility — say, a good-sized multiple-family property — in which the total amount of up-front cash is more than you'd want from a single partner who may get nervous just because of the amount. You might say, "This may be bigger than the two of us should try to handle alone. Do you know anybody who might want to join us in this great investment?"

Be sure every partnership you form is backed by a clear written agreement, not only a partnership agreement but a management agreement as well. You've heard the old saying: There are just two times when partners fight — when they're making money and when they're losing money.

Be sure that the partners understand that your principal contributions are coming up with the deal and managing it. You don't want a dissatisfied partner saying to you, months down the road, "I put up all the money and you get two-thirds of the income." What I'm driving at here is the core of successful partnerships. When you hold back information or try to shave the truth, you're inviting disaster. You can show partners how their money will generate more money without resorting to duplicity or half-truths. My graduate course on partnerships entitled "Creating Quick Wealth With Partners" is available through the Professional Education Institute.

PERFECTING YOUR TELEPHONE PERSONALITY

You certainly have noticed, when you call an individual or a business office, how the voice of the person answering the phone, and what that person says, affects your own mood and opinion.

Some people answer the phone in a laconic way. They sound bored even though they may not be. Others answer tersely — "Yep?" or "Jones here" or "Hello," spoken the way General Patton might have growled hello to one of his troops.

An absolute rule of phone manners: Pleasantry pays off.

So even though you have a headache or were up late or just had one of your pending deals fall through, make every call the first call of the day. You're rarin' to go. You've shaken off whatever negatives may have clouded your sunny temperament. You're thinking and acting the way a successful executive should.

That goes for your telephone answering device too. Remember an absolute rule of business negotiation:

Action dictates reaction.

That means if the message you record onto your machine is cold-blooded and impersonal, the message the caller will leave will be cold-blooded and impersonal. If your message is warm and friendly, the message you'll get will be warm and friendly. In fact, people who may be calling to complain or raise an objection somehow lose their indignation when a friendly telephone voice greets them.

One additional caveat:

Don't get cute on your answering device. I've winced at answering devices that included fake dog-barks, maniacal laughter, and infants saying "Daddy and Mommy aren't here now, but if you'll leave your name and number at the beep . . ." You're in business. Pleasant, always. Confident, always. Professional, always. Cute, never.

One additional point: Three words too many people are afraid to speak are "I don't know." Why is that? We aren't expected to know everything. In fact, professing *not* to know can often bring a positive reaction.

So if a seller asks a question you can't answer, don't be afraid to say, "That's one terrific question, and I have to admit I don't know the answer. Let me find out." I've found that the more successful an executive is, the less worried he or she is about admitting there's something he or she doesn't know.

Am I right or am I wrong in making that statement? Is your answer, "I don't know"? See how easy, natural, and correct it is?

CHAPTER SIXTEEN

The End of This Book . . . But You're Just Getting Started!

(Suggestion: Admiral David Farragut achieved immortality through a single sentence he hurled at his crew at Mobile Bay, during the War Between the States: "Damn the torpedoes! Full speed ahead!" Long before Farragut, Shakespeare had a marvelous line in his play Henry VI: "Delays have dangerous ends." And fifteen hundred years before Shakespeare, the Roman statesman Lucan pronounced a great profundity: "Delay is ever fatal to those who are prepared." I still remember a joke from my school days: "The Procrastination Society will have its Monday morning meeting on Friday evening instead of Wednesday afternoon."

I'm reminding you of these because — assuming you've read through this book, underlined and highlighted relevant passages, maybe made some notes on the margin, and understood the principles — you're ready to swing into action. Lucan was right: Delay is ever fatal to those who are prepared. (You're prepared. Don't become a fatality.))

SET UP A TIMETABLE

Let's understand each other.

Delay can be fatal because each day you delay causes your enthusiasm to become a little more stale. But don't try to conquer the world the first day. Set up a logical timetable.

An important realization is that, starting out, you won't have the knowledge and confidence you'll have after you've made half a dozen deals. Of course that's true, and we've already discussed it. We've also discussed the importance of appearing to be confident. You can balance the initial lack of experience with the aura of confidence by

Carleton, I'm 27 years old. I never thought I'd own 11 houses — never — let alone do it in about six months. I make over $20,000 a year from them, and I'm just starting. The fun thing is I've taken the principles I've learned from your course and used them to help friends and family buy *their* own homes and properties.
— *Robert Lederer, Missouri*

looking, originally, for some basic deals — foreclosures and "motivated buyer" ads . . . "Moving, must sell" situations . . . as many "no money down" offers as you can make without delving into unsavory neighborhoods or lapsing into an emotion-driven "Gotta make this deal" attitude.

I'm assuming you're pre-armed with some credit cards or an elementary line of credit. If you haven't jumped over that hurdle, make it your first order of business. (Before you do, re-read chapter 5.)

I propose a three-month "revving up" period. No, it isn't a "learning" period. Your whole life, as mine, is a learning period. It's a period during which you add increments to your real estate knowledge . . . kind of a post-graduate course. The concept is based on your having five to seven hours a week to devote to real estate investing. That's an hour a day or less.

We're back to Coué's Law, mentioned earlier in this text: *"Day by day, in every way, I'm getting better and better."* As you wake up in the morning, make a commitment that by the time you go to bed, you'll have achieved something! When you go to bed that night, ask yourself what you've achieved.

WHAT TO DO *RIGHT NOW:*

Are you ready to get moving?

You are if you've followed the advice in the early chapters. You have at least one valid credit card . . . preferably two. You're calling, or writing letters, to the credit card companies, asking for an increased credit line. (While you're at it, ask them to eliminate any annual fee they're charging you.)

You've been negotiating a credit line and overdraft protection with your bank. No, no, no — don't use this as an excuse to delay. That's what it would be, a delay. You certainly can launch your real estate investing career without a credit line.

Strangely, many people use lack of a credit line with their bank as an excuse. Don't be one of them. Strange, also, is the fact that many people actually fear walking into a bank and discussing their circumstance with a bank officer. Don't be one of them, either. Banks are in business to make money available. As pointed out so often, apparent confidence is a major key not only to rapport but to getting what you want.

Do you have business cards? If you don't, make *today* the day you order them. No stalling. Your occupation on the card? Real estate investor! And don't cheat on the quantity. Print enough cards so you won't feel you're running short when you pass them out liberally . . . which is exactly what you should do.

Today is start-up day! Don't wait until tomorrow.

MONTH NUMBER ONE: THE START-UP

During your first month as a real estate investor, you'll find it highly beneficial to visit a couple of title companies. You have two goals: First, you want to be on a first-name basis with some of the people there. You need title insurance on every property you buy, and even though the seller usually pays the cost of a title search, the title company can be a helpful comrade. Over a lunch or in a casual "How's it going today?" phone call, you can get a feeling for what kinds of property are selling fast, what kinds are "dogs," and how the overall market is shaping up.

Second, a title company has its finger on the pulse of the real estate "world" in your area. A title company has the capability of handling escrow money, and taking care of many of the details of a closing, and obtaining copies of deeds and mortgages at a nominal cost. Their employees are in the courthouse every day, requesting and picking up documents. What a big a time-saver it is for you if they'll work your request in with theirs, and do so for a nominal fee.

You'll be glad you have that relationship with some title companies when you're closing your first deal. Here's a friendly face and a "How are ya!" — a colleague instead of a stranger.

Cultivating title companies may not in itself make deals for you . . . but you never know. A title company employee is often the first to know when somebody else's deal has fallen through and the seller is getting a bit desperate.

What positively *will* make deals for you is another first-month activity: Choose three or four neighborhoods and make them your "stomping grounds." Find out everything you can about them — schools, transportation, whether single-family or multi-family residences are most common, how many properties are rented and their rent rates, and how many "For Sale" signs have sprouted on front lawns.

You'll quickly get an accurate feeling for what homes in each neighborhood should sell for. Then, when you're strolling or driving or even biking through one of your chosen neighborhoods, when you see a homeowner standing in front of a home that has a "For Sale" sign, you can stop and begin a casual negotiation then and there. You may not close a deal that day, but I can tell you from many, many experiences, that I've left business cards with people who called me weeks and months later, asking if I was still interested and would I make an offer.

Starting today, spend at least half an hour a day with the real estate classified ads. These are your bread and butter, the source of constant replenishment.

Highlight or circle the ads that seem to fall inside the parameters you've set up. Call them. Don't be afraid to ask questions to qualify each property, especially if you use the principles you've read in chapter 7. Once you've qualified the property, arrange to visit it.

Visiting unqualified properties is the biggest and most frustrating waste of time any real estate investor can get tangled in. Here's a perfect example of what can happen when emotion rules over logic: You've gone a whole week without finding a property that matches your standards. So you lower your standards. Result: Time wasted. Don't let this happen.

As has been pointed out many times in this text, the relationship between real estate investors and real estate brokers is a tenuous one. Brokers can be the strongest source of leads and deals you'll ever find . . . or they can be antagonists. Much of the determination as to which they become is the result of *your* approach.

Warning: If you say to a broker, "I'm looking to buy some property with no money down," forget it. Not only are you scarred with the mark of Cain; the broker may pass the word to associates that you want to pick up property by making no investment in it, possibly even depriving the broker of an immediate commission. So when a broker asks you how much cash you have to invest — and I grant you, that's a pretty crass (although logical) question for the broker to ask — smile and answer, "Whatever it takes."

Now the most important move during the first month: Make at least four offers on properties. Understand what has to be behind this: To make four offers, you should have looked at and analyzed at least 20 properties. *Not one* of those offers should take place as a result of your thinking, "He said four, and I only have three, so I'll make an offer on this one even though it doesn't quite qualify."

I suggest that during the first month you not become involved in complicated transactions. Make all four "no money down" offers, unless another opportunity, a more complex one, pops up and you feel capable of handling it. If you follow the rest of the directions for Month One, you not only won't have any problem finding four properties on which you'll make an offer; your problem may be culling down to four. Wait! Why cull? I said *at least* four. And remember, no money down does *not* mean that the seller gets no cash at close. It just doesn't have to come out of your pocket.

And if every offer you make gets turned down or falls through? In two words, "So what?"

MONTH NUMBER TWO: SHIFTING INTO A HIGHER GEAR

Now you're in business. You're aggressively looking for property. In fact, you're perfectly willing to offer your contacts a $100 bill for leads they refer to you, if you eventually buy.

Stay in touch with your banker. Your position, your rapport, and your "clout," get stronger by the month. Drop by from time to time, just to say "hello." Share clippings from publications you have read relating to banking and real estate, ones in which you think the banker may be interested. Don't be a pest; be a businessperson.

Start cultivating potential partners and co-investors. Have breakfast or lunch with at least two of them. Don't sell — it's executive to executive, businessperson to businessperson. Your attitude has to reflect what has to be the truth: It's a profitable move for both of you or neither one of you wants to go ahead.

> *The rule of success couldn't be simpler: If you do not make offers, you will not buy properties. Circling and highlighting newspaper ads is an academic exercise unless you act on those circles and highlights.*

You should be comfortable with your posture as a real estate investor. That means you can start seeking out properties beyond basic no-money-down offers. This month, you should make at least eight offers.

We've bought three properties in the Los Angeles area in about six months, all with NO MONEY DOWN. We have an extra $11,000 to spend each year (which paid off our cars and all our bills). Our credit is great now. Our net worth is now up to $120,000. Your course has changed our lives incredibly. We're so glad we learned about your system.

— *George and Latecia Lee, California*

At no point should the adjective "discouraged" apply to you. One strong deal can make the year . . . and we've had far too many success stories, from people who didn't have five seconds of prior experience when they began studying the same materials you have, to believe that you can't quickly spurt to ownership of a whole bunch of properties. And even more comforting to you should be the fact that many of them had zero cash and no credit.

Every couple of days, re-read five or ten pages of this book, chosen at random. You'll constantly find new ideas and procedures, plus reminders of those you may have forgotten or have been overlooking. Too, you will find that you are "remotivated."

MONTH NUMBER THREE: YOU'RE SOLIDLY IN BUSINESS

By the time the third month rolls around, you have a strong group of contacts — in the neighborhoods you've selected, among real estate investors, agents, and bankers, and with people who now know you're in a position to make an offer on properties that are available or (even better!) about to become available.

Expand your territory. Start looking around in neighborhoods adjacent to the ones you originally chose.

Let's see if your banking connection is ready to pay off. Go into the bank and try to borrow some money. Notice, please, I said *try to borrow,* not *borrow.* If the bank turns you down, don't worry about it. You have plenty of deals available to you without bank money, and once the bank knows how you're doing, they'll come to you.

This month you should make a minimum of twelve offers. And that really is the minimum. You really might be able to make two or three offers each day . . . but the number of offers is tied to the amount of time you're allocating to real estate investing.

Don't slow down. Don't say to yourself, "I made a deal today so I can slack off." Don't say to yourself, "I'm just not making deals, so I'll wait until the market is better," or,

I've been in the military for over 13 years — always away from my family. I wanted to find something that would let me see my kids grow up. I also had been burdened with an unfortunate bankruptcy. Using your real estate system, my wife Yvette and I now have a net worth of $589,000 and $60,000 annual cash flow. The amazing thing is, between traveling and being stationed away from home, I've done all this in only 10 actual months of investing. Now I'm basically retired, making triple what I made in the army. I know it would take me a lifetime to have this kind of wealth by investing in IRA's and putting cash away. I'm 33 years old and I feel my family is financially set for life! I am very appreciative.

— Ed Trittel, Georgia

"This is not for me." Keep that tempo going, and don't be de-railed by occasional turndowns. Nobody bats one thousand. Remember Rudyard Kipling's line? "We have forty million excuses for failure, but not a single reason."

WANT TO *REALLY* GET INTO THIS?

What's next on the docket?

First item: Congratulations!

You've made it through the book. How great an accomplishment is this? Well, I can't answer that. Only you can. I am absolutely and positively convinced that you *should* be able to buy property and make money as a real estate investor. I also am very much aware that some will read this book, nod "Yeah, sure," and never lift a finger to increase their income and net worth by hundreds of thousands of dollars or even more.

With the information you'll use from this book, you certainly can buy a home with no money down. You certainly can expand to other properties. You certainly can (and should) generate a comfortable income. The tool is right here; in your hands; this very second.

Obviously, a book can't be as extensive nor as intensive as a more personal presentation. The complete home study course includes many video and audio cassettes, a text somewhat paralleling this one, but considerably expanded and with additional refinements. It also has a legal forms portfolio that contains full-sized forms that you can copy and fax. These forms are all buyer-oriented, unlike those available from a real estate agent or the so-called "standard" forms you might purchase from an office supply store.

The complete course does have some additional advantages. Because it's built around video and audiocassettes, or, if you prefer, compact discs (CDs), taped during an actual series of sessions, you can refresh your mind as you're driving your car, lounging on the beach, or relaxing in your living room. The cassettes offer some interplay with those attending the seminar. They're easy listening.

You might want to move to an even higher plateau. If so, three additional courses are available to you, also at the special price reserved for those who have already invested in this book. The Professional Education institute calls these the "Investor's Success Series."

Volume I is "The Painless Guide to Profitable Property Management." Volume II is "Cashing In on Foreclosures and Distressed Properties: A Step by Step Formula." Volume III is "Creating Quick Wealth with Partners." Each of the courses contains a step-by-step manual and six audiocassette tapes.

I recommend these "post-graduate" cassettes if you want to make a big killing in real estate. Some of my students who use all the methods (and none of them are difficult) have become multimillionaires. (Note: If you choose to invest in any or all of my real estate home study courses, know that if you're not satisfied for any reason, you may return the course, within 30 days, for a full refund, no questions asked.)

As I say, it's up to you. To get started, you need only one asset other than the book you have in your hands — the commitment to succeed. If averages mean anything at all, apply the principles you've learned and bingo! You certainly should buy your first property within 50 days.

Want to retire from your present occupation and become a full-time real estate investor? You're on your way. Want to retire at the end of your business career, as a millionaire? You're on your way to that, too.

I've said it many times to students all over the country: "My world is better because real estate came my way. I hope that someday you'll say your world is better because I came your way."

Epilogue

You've now discovered some of the creative techniques I, and others, have used to gain wealth through real estate.

You've learned that success as a real estate investor knows no limits. It crosses gender, race, age and geographical boundaries. It doesn't care whether you live in a small town in the Midwest and speak with an accent or are a student living in a metropolitan area.

And, you know that I did not grow up with money. So, as a final testimonial, I'd like to tell you what my success has done for and to me: Financial success has not only brought me the "toys" of life for which we all dream and crave, but a very strong self esteem and self confidence as well. I now have a place in the whole scheme of things that I truly relish.

You see, I am now in a position to help others achieve what I have attained — and to light the path through my personal experience. I truly want to help you achieve your goals — to become financially independent.

Throughout this book, you've been exposed to some of the learning materials, courses, videos and investing systems available through the Professional Education Institute. These learning tools are there for you when you feel you need them. Put them to good use — and I hope to see your picture, letter and success story among those I'll be including in the next edition of this book.

Best wishes for continued success!

— Carleton H. Sheets

**For more information
please call this toll-free number:
1-800-369-6314
or visit us at our website:
www.carltonsheets.com**

Appendix

CREDIT REPORTS

Most people are not aware that information about their credit history is collected and stored in credit bureaus across the country. There are three major credit bureaus that act as clearing houses for collecting information concerning everyone's payment habits. Smaller bureaus receive their reports from these large credit bureaus. Potential lenders and businesses can contact their local bureaus to receive a report about you to help them decide if you are a good credit risk.

Typically, a report contains personal information (such as your address, phone number, job title or description, and marital status), payment schedules for loans and credit purchases, applications for credit, lawsuits, bankruptcies, and debts. Any information more than seven years old cannot be included. The exception to this rule is a bankruptcy which stays in your file for up to ten years.

Credit bureaus do not verify or make value judgments about information they collect. It is up to lenders to decide, based on their own criteria, whether or not to give you credit. That is why it is so important to make sure that your credit file is accurate.

Write to the three major credit bureaus and ask them for a copy of your credit report. Their addresses are as follows: *(Please note, these addresses change often.)*

TransUnion Corp.
P. O. Box 390
Springfield, PA 19064-0390
(800) 916-8880

Equifax Information Service Center
P. O. Box 105873
Atlanta, GA 30348-5873
(800) 685-1111

Experian
P. O. Box 2106
Allen, TX 75013-2106
(800) 643-3334

When you write to these companies, you must include your current name and address (if you have been at your present address for less than five years, show your previous address), your Social Security number, your date of birth, and, while not required, a copy of a photo I.D. such as a driver's license. This would probably expedite your request.

By law, credit bureaus must show your credit file to you and tell you who, if anyone, has asked for your file in the last six months. If you have tried to borrow money within the past 30 days and have been turned down for the loan, the credit bureau probably will not charge you to look at your file. Charges may also depend on the state you live in. Credit bureaus can charge up to $8 for a copy of your credit report.

A sample of a credit report, and an explanation on how to read it, is on the following pages.

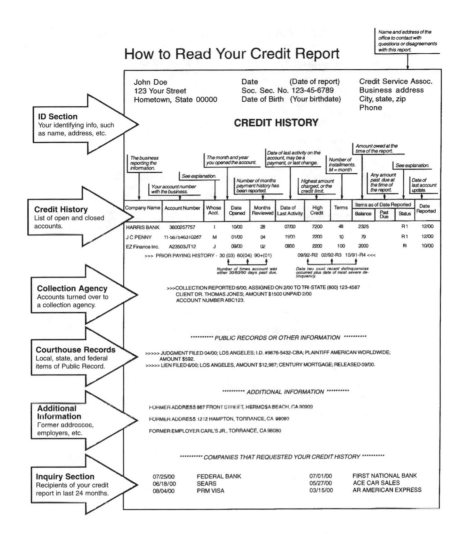

How to Read Your Credit Report

Sample Credit Report
This is typical information included on a credit report. Information more than seven years old cannot be included except in the case of bankruptcy which stays in your file for up to ten years.

How to Read Your Credit Report (Continued)

WHOSE ACCOUNT

Indicates who is responsible for the account and the type of participation you have with the account.

J = Joint
U = Undesignated
I = Individual
A = Authorized user
T = Terminated
M = Maker
C = Co-Maker / Co-Signer
B = On behalf of another person
S = Shared

STATUS
(Type of Account)

O = Open
    (entire balance due each month)

R = Revolving
    (payment amount variable)

I = Installment
    (fixed number of payments)

TIMELINESS OF PAYMENT

0 = Approved not used; too new to rate

1 = Paid as agreed

2 = 30 + days past due

3 = 60 + days past due

4 = 90 + days past due

5 = Pays or paid 120 + days past the due date; or collection account

6 = Making regular payments under wage earner plan or similar arrangement

7 = Repossession

8 = Charged off to bad debt

INQUIRIES NOT REPORTED TO BUSINESSES:

PRM. This type of inquiry means that only your name and address were given to a credit grantor so they could offer you an application for credit. (PRM inquiries remain for six months.*)

AM or **AR.** These inquiries indicate a periodic review of your credit history by one of your creditors. (AM and AR inquiries remain for 6 months.*)

ACIS or **UPDATE.** These inquiries indicate credit reporting service activity in response to your contact with us for either a copy of your credit report or a request for research.

PRM, AM, AR, ACIS and **UPDATE** inquiries do not show on credit reports that businesses receive, only on copies provided to you.

* 12 months for Connecticut residents.

Explanation of Codes
There are codes in the credit report that are defined in this chart. The codes are often included on the first side of the credit report but are expanded here for clarity.

SELLER INFORMATION FORM

Seller: ☐ Good ☐ Flexible
☐ Rejected ☐ Inflexible

Source or Lead: _____

Property Address: _____ Date:_____

_____ Phone:_____

1. Seller's Name _____

2. Property

    A. Size (sq. ft.) _____

    B. Total Rooms _____

    C. Layout_____ Bedrooms _____ Baths: Full ____ Half ____

    D. Lot Size _____

    E. Garage _____ Size_____

    F. Special Features _____

    G. Appliances, etc. _____

3. Price: $ _____

4. Existing Financing

    A. Assumable _____

    B. Lender_____ Amount $ _____

    C. Payment: Current _____ Amount $ _____

5. Will seller assist financing? _____ Cash needed? _____

6. How long on market? _____

7. How long owned? _____

8. Why selling? _____

9. Like most?_____ Like least? _____

10. Renters in neighborhood?_____ Rent rates?_____

11. Lease / Option?_____

12. Cash Deal, Quick Close Price $ _____

13. Broker Involved:

Name: _____ Phone: _____

Background: _____

Could manage?_____

Rental Value $ _____ Vacancy Rate _____

Any other good investment properties? _____

PROPERTY ANALYSIS FORM

1. OWNERSHIP AND PROPERTY LOCATION

Owner's Name _____ Telephone _____

Owner's Address _____

Property Address _____

2. PHYSICAL DESCRIPTION

Size in Square Feet _____ Bedrooms _____ Baths: Full __ Half __

Appliances   Refrigerator _____ Stove _____ Oven _____

                 Washer/Dryer _____ Water Softener _____

                 Microwave _____ Garbage Disposal _____

                 Dishwasher _____ Other _____

Basement _____ Attic _____ Porch _____ Utility Room _____

Garage _____ Den/Family Room _____ Lot Size _____ Zoning _____

Fireplace _____ Window Coverings _____

Carpet _____ Construction _____ Age _____

Central AC _____ Heat _____ Largest Utility Bill _____

City Water/Septic _____ School District _____

Public Transportation _____ Taxes _____

Comments _____

3. OWNER'S SITUATION

How Long Owned? _____ How Long On Market? _____ Asking Price _____

Original Asking Price _____ Date of Price Change _____

Why Selling? _____ Needs Cash _____

How Much Cash? _____ Could Cash Be Spread Over Time? _____

What Owner Will Be Doing With Cash Received _____

Will Owner Assist In Financing? _____ How Much? _____

Interest Rate _____

What Owner Likes Most About Property _____ Least _____

Comments _____

4. RENTAL ANALYSIS

Is Property Rented Now _____ To Whom? _____ Children? ___ Pets? ___

How Long? _____ Lease Or Month To Month? _____

Monthly Rent _____ Last Increase _____ Last Month's Rent _____

Security Deposit _____ Concessions _____

Potential Rental Income _____ Improvements Needed Before Renting _____

_____

Other Rents In Neighborhood _____ Rent Paid _____

Comments _____

5. FINANCING

First Mortgage   Lender _____ Balance _____

                 Interest Rate _____ Assumable _____ Payment _____

                 P.I.T.* _____ Constant _____

Second Mortgage Lender _____ Balance _____

                 Interest Rate _____ Assumable _____ Payment _____

                 Constant _____

Other Liens _____

                              *Principal, Interest, Taxes, and Insurance

Glossary

A

Acceleration Clause

A clause in a mortgage that allows the balance of the note to be called due and payable by the lender, if the legal or equitable title to a property is passed.

Addendum

An addition to a pre-printed contract form. Usually contains terms and conditions not covered in the form. Sometimes referred to as a rider.

Amenities

Items adding to one's comfort, convenience, use or enjoyment of a property, such as a walk-in closet, a fire-alarm system, an in ground swimming pool, or a fenced-in yard.

Appreciation

An increase in the value of a property over a period of time. This occurs as a result of inflation, and/or escalating demand and/or possible improvements to a property.

Appreciation Table	A table showing the value of a property at some future date based on varying rates of appreciation.
Assumable Loan	A mortgage loan that may be transferred from one borrower to another without having to meet the standards of a lender. It is also known as a non-qualifying assumption.

B

Bankruptcy	A legal process wherein a person or other legal entity is determined to be unable to pay their debts and obligations. There are several forms (Chapters) of bankruptcy ranging from complete elimination of assets and debts to the reorganization of debt.
Bread and Butter Property	A home that is utilized by and appeals to the largest portion to perspective single family tenants and owners.

C

Cash Back	Money received by a BUYER at a closing when acquiring a property.
Cash Flow	Effective gross income minus operating expenses and payments for debt (debt service). Also known as cash throw-off.
Closing	The point in the process of buying and selling a property when the title passes to the buyer and the seller receives payment.

Collateral

Real or personal property pledged as security for the repayment of a debt.

Constructive Asset

A possession that increases in value over the period of ownership.

Consumer Price Index

A comparison of retail prices of a predetermined group of consumer goods and services from one time period to another.

Contract For Deed

A contract for the sale of a property wherein the seller is obligated to transfer marketable title to the buyer after the buyer has paid for a portion or all of the property. The payment is usually made in installments. (Also known as a Land Contract or Agreement for Deed.)

Conventional Financing

Loans secured from customary sources such as commercial banks, savings banks or credit unions. Most have consistent borrower qualification requirements.

Cosmetic Repairs

Those repairs that can be accomplished without a building permit. This includes landscaping, interior and exterior painting and carpet and/or appliance replacement.

Creative Buyers

A buyer who invents creative ways to acquire and pay for properties that would otherwise not be available to him or her.

Credit Rating

An estimation of an individual's future performance as a borrower based on information from a report provided by an information agency. The report in large part is a credit history of the individual.

D

Debt Partner	A partner that lends money to a venture. Does not participate directly in management or profit and losses.
Debt Service	The payment necessary to meet all debt obligations on a property; usually includes principal and interest.
Deed	A legal instrument reflecting ownership of real estate.
Depreciation	A bookkeeping concept allowing the owner of an income producing asset to receive income tax consideration for the theoretical decrease in value of the asset caused by wear, deterioration and obsolescence. This is available even when a property may be going up in value.
Destructive Asset	An asset which will immediately decrease in market value once it is purchased, for example, clothes or an automobile.
"Due On Sale" Clause	See acceleration clause.

E

Effective Gross Income	Income from all sources minus adjustments for vacancy and collection losses.
Equitable Title	Ownership that is, by contract, contingent upon the occurrence of a stipulated future event.

Equity	The difference between the fair market value of a property and the debt owed on it.
Equity Build-Up	The reduction in the mortgage amount due as result of principal payments over time (amortization).
Equity Partner	An individual who owns a part of a piece of real estate and who participates in the profits and losses of the endeavor, and possibly the management as well.
Exchange	A provision in the Internal Revenue Service code that permits trading like-kind properties without incurring capital gains tax obligations on the property given up.

F

Federal Housing	The agencies that fall under the Department of Housing and Urban Development that, among other things, administer federal mortgage insurance and other housing programs.
Financial Analysis	Determining, on a pro-forma basis (the probable form it will take), the economic viability of a transaction once all financial information has been received.
Flexible Seller	A seller who finds any terms and conditions that meet his needs are acceptable; one who is highly motivated to sell because of personal circumstance.

Flexible Terms	Contract and financing terms that are neither traditional nor standard.
Flip	To purchase a property and immediately resell it or sell it after rehabilitation.
Foreclosure	A highly regulated procedure whereby the lender under the terms of a loan in default, gains title to the property collateralizing the loan. The property is usually auctioned off at public sale.
Free and Clear Property	A property that is completely unencumbered by loans of record or other debt.

G

Grantee	One who obtains title to real property by deed. (The purchaser)
Grantor	One who conveys title to real property by deed.
Gross Income	Income from all sources from a property. Includes rent, laundry receipts, fines, pool fees, late charges, recreational equipment income, etc.

H

Home Study Course	"How to Buy Your First Home or Investment Property With No Down Payment" by Carleton H. Sheets.

I

Interest Rate

The agreed upon amount a borrower must pay to a lender to compensate the lender for the use of the money and risk.

Investor

One who alone or with others, invests in income producing real estate.

J

Junior Lien

A mortgage or other encumbrance, junior to a senior lien or mortgage.

L

Lease-Option

A transaction wherein the owner of a property leases it to a lessee (tenant) and in so doing gives the lessee the right to buy the property at some predetermined future date at a stipulated or formulated price.

Letter of Intent

A non-binding letter stating a perspective buyer's intent to buy a property, usually for a certain price but with terms that are general rather than specific.

Leverage

The borrowing of money in connection with a real estate investment. If 50 percent of the cost is borrowed, the leverage is 50 percent. If 100 percent of the amount is borrowed (no money down), the leverage is 100 percent.

Listing	A contract in which a property owner gives a licensed agent the written authorization to act on his behalf to sell a property.

M

Market Interest Rate	The going rate of interest being charged for similar loans in a given market area.
Market Place	A demographically homogenous grouping of similar homes that are usually bounded by natural or man-made barriers (e.g. tollways, bridges, rivers, main thoroughfares).
Market Value	The value of a home that is established by the recent selling prices for similar properties in the area.
Mortgage	A contract granting the lender certain rights in the event the borrower defaults on the note the mortgage secures. It gives the lender the right to foreclose on the property.
Mortgagee	The lender who receives the mortgage from the borrower to collateralize a loan.
Mortgagor	The borrower who gives the mortgage to the lender to collateralize the loan he has received.
Multiple Listing Service	A service offered by a local Board of Realtors, where members share listings. Each Realtor has access to the listings of every other board member.

Multiple Offer	Two or more different offers on the same property are offered simultaneously by a buyer, giving the seller an option of which offer to accept.

N

Net-Net Purchase	The buyer pays the seller a set amount for his property and pays all of the closing costs as well. The seller knows the exact amount he or she will receive at the closing.
Net Operating Income (N.O.I.)	Adjusted gross income minus operating expenses but excluding debt service (mortgage payments). It is the budget for debt.
Net Worth	The total value of an individual's assets minus that person's debts.
Nonessential Contingencies	Contract contingencies inserted by either or both parties to be used as bargaining chips in later negotiations.
Note	An instrument that evidences a debt. A mortgage loan consists of a note (finance instrument) given by the borrower to the lender and the mortgage (security instrument) also given to the lender in exchange for the loan.

O

Offer Form	A form, usually preprinted, on which offers to purchase real estate are made. Until accepted by the seller they are only offers. Once accepted, it becomes a contact.

Option	An instrument giving the right to a party to lease or purchase a property over a specified time period for specified consideration. It is binding for the optionor (seller) but not the optionee (buyer).

P

Partnership Agreement	A written agreement between partners which outlines their respective responsibilities and liabilities.
Point	One percent of the principal amount of a mortgage loan, usually charged to the borrower as a loan origination fee by the lender.
Positive Cash Flow	The amount of income remaining after payment of all operating expenses and debt service. (See also Cash Throw-Off and Cash Flow)
Principal	The outstanding balance of a debt upon which an interest payment is calculated. This amount is usually reduced monthly by the principal portion of a mortgage payment.
Puffery	Exaggerated praise of a product or property.

Q

Qualifying For a Loan	A procedure whereby a lender critiques certain elements of a prospective borrower's financial status to determine that person's credit worthiness.

Quit Claim Deed

A document that transfers the ownership interest, if any, a grantor might have in a property.

R

Real Estate Investor

One who purchases property with the anticipation of income through the use of property.

*Real Estate
Speculator*

Anticipates profits through the buying and selling of properties.

S

Selling Right

Obtaining the highest possible price from the sale of property.

T

Tax Benefits, Shelters

The artificial paper losses created due to depreciation or cost recovery, that are in excess of the income produced by a property. These artificial losses can sometimes be used to offset other taxable income earned by the owners. In general, a shelter is any deferral, reduction, or elimination of a tax due.

Tenant Check Service

A fee service that investigates and reports on all aspects of a perspective tenant's life to help a landlord evaluate that person's worthiness as a tenant.

Title Company	A company that searches the public records for information regarding the title to real estate. Most title companies also insure against claims against titles once the search is completed.

U

Unilateral Contract	A contract that is binding only on one party. For example, an option which binds only the seller (optionor).

V

Department of Veteran's Affairs	A department of the federal government that administers a program that guarantees the repayment of mortgage loans made to veterans.

W

Wraparound Mortgage	A mortgage held by the seller/mortgagee. The buyer/mortgagor pays the seller/mortgagee the debt service on the wraparound mortgage and the seller/mortgagee continues to pay the debt service on the underlying or original mortgage(s).

Z

Zoning	Laws which regulate and control how a property may be used. Purchasing a property who's use is not in conformity with zoning laws could result in penalties or at best, a severe reduction in the value of a property.

Index